Jewish Science

Divine Healing in Judaism

Jewish Science

Divine Healing in Judaism

With Special Reference
to the Jewish Scriptures
and Prayerbook

by

Alfred Geiger Moses

Edited
by
William F. Shannon

Hudson Mohawk Press
Latham, NY

Hudson Mohawk Press
595 New Loudon Road #138
Latham, New York 12110

www.hudsonmohawkpress.com

This edited edition published by Hudson Mohawk Press in January 2011.
Jewish Science was originally self-published by Alfred Geiger Moses in
1916 in Mobile, Alabama.

ISBN 978-0-9843040-3-5 (paperback)

Library of Congress Control Number: 2011920030

Editing and book design by William F. Shannon

Printed in the United States

CONTENTS

Editor's Note to the 2011 Edition   i

Foreword to the 1916 Edition   v

Chapter 1
The Principle of Divine Healing   1

Chapter 2
The Chasidic Movement   11

Chapter 3
The Change of Name   25

Chapter 4
Jewish Science vs. Christian Science   29

Chapter 5
A Refutal of Anti-Jewish References in "Science and Health"   39

Chapter 6
A Complete Anthology of Jewish Science   59

Index of Biblical Passages   122

EDITOR'S NOTE

William F. Shannon

Long before the blockbuster 2006 movie and bestselling book *The Secret* by Rhonda Byrne, and long before Esther and Jerry Hicks' *Law of Attraction* and the many other books in the same vein, there were the original works of the New Thought Movement in the late 19th and early 20th century. The majority of New Thought works came out of the Christian tradition, such as William Walker Atkinson's seminal work, *Thought Vibration or the Law of Attraction in the Thought World*, which is available in a new edited edition from Hudson Mohawk Press, and Mary Baker Eddy's *Science and Health with Key to the Scriptures*, which to this day is the textbook of the Christian Science churches. The works of New Thought struck a cord with spiritual seekers of all religious traditions, including Judaism, and planted the seed out of which all other 20th century works on positive thinking were to grow, either directly or indirectly.

Thousands of American Jews were drawn to Christian Science and other New Thought teachings at

the turn of the 20th century along with countless
Christians. The growing popularity of New Thought
teachings among American Jews concerned Jewish
leaders of the time, including American Reform Rabbi
Alfred Geiger Moses, who decided to do something
about it. Seeing much in New Thought teachings that
could be adapted to Judaism, once stripped of its
Christian elements, Rabbi Moses first published
Jewish Science in 1916. He spends much time
showing that the precepts of Christian Science and
other New Thought denominations are drawn largely
from the Hebrew scriptures.

The reader should be aware when reading the
present volume that the author of *Jewish Science*
assumes the superiority of the Jewish religion
throughout his discussion, focusing on the notion of
the "Chosen People" and the fact that later religious
writings have often drawn on the Hebrew scriptures.
Rabbi Moses's religio-centrism should not take away
from the otherwise valuable insights in his text. His
defensiveness is understandable in the context of his
critique of Mary Baker Eddy's *Science and Health
with Key to the Scriptures*, the foundation text of
Christian Science. Moses went to great pains to show
where he thought Christian Science went wrong when
it came to Divine Healing.

Alfred Geiger Moses would go on to produce a
revised and expanded edition of *Jewish Science* in
1920. We have chosen to produce this new edition of
the 1916 version because it is the version most close
in time and thinking to the New Thought teachings out
of which the Rabbi's thinking grew. Some might say
that the 1920 edition went to great pains to needlessly
expand beyond the elegant simplicity of the original,
without adding much of importance to it. The Jewish

Science of Rabbi Alfred Geiger Moses led to the spiritual awakening of many apathetic American Jews, giving them an alternative to Christian Science and other New Thought denominations, based in their own religious tradition. The scripture citations in this little book serve a very valuable purpose in directing readers to Bible passages in the Hebrew scriptures that support and enrich a New Thought point of view.

Hudson Mohawk Press is pleased to make available this new, redesigned edition of the earliest version of *Jewish Science* as a contribution to the continuing search for Truth, in the hope that the positive thought vibrations of the author will reach a new generation of readers, who we hope will take what they want from this classic work, and leave behind for others that which may not work for them.

* * * *

WILLIAM F. SHANNON is the Publisher and Editor of Hudson Mohawk Press. He holds a Master of Arts in Integrated Studies/Cultural Studies from Athabasca University in Canada.

FOREWORD
to the 1916 Edition

The term, "Jewish Science," will on first blush seem strange and startling to the average reader, for inevitably it will suggest the well known phrase, "Christian Science." I have purposely used the much mooted term Science, because to the religious mind it has come to connote the entire subject of Divine Healing. Yet, the Jewish student knows full well, that the word is an exact translation of the Hebrew term, often found in the Jewish Scriptures. I mean the word *Chochmoh* which means, "Divine Wisdom" or "Science." Therefore, the word Science in a religious sense is strictly Jewish in its origin, and the entire phrase, "Jewish Science" is thoroughly in keeping with the Faith and History of Judaism. The Jewish Bible abounds in passages, dealing with the favorite theme of *Chochmoh* or Wisdom. The Book of Proverbs contains several classic texts which describe the working of this principle. All such passages will be found in full in Chapter Six, entitled, "A Complete Anthology of Jewish Science."

Now, that I have justified the use of the term Jewish Science, let me set forth just what is meant by this expression. Jewish Science deals with *the entire subject of Divine Healing as it is unfolded in the Literature* and *History of the Jewish People.* Many Jews are unaware of the fact that their Religion teaches Faith-Cure, and unfortunately have turned to Christian Science to discover the truth of Divine Healing. The result is that in this country the new cult has drawn many Sons and Daughters of the Covenant away from their ancient faith. One object in writing this book is to reach this class of Jews, who through ignorance of their faith and literature have deserted the Synagogue. I hope to prove to them that *the art or principle of Divine Healing has been known in Judaism* for thousands of years, and that there still exists a real Jewish Science Cult or Sect, the Chasidim of Europe. Above all, in this work, I will conclusively show that the Jewish Bible contains many texts and passages, teaching the power of God to heal the ills that flesh is heir to. In fact, the Jewish Scriptures contain the first and original message on Divine Healing. It is well known that Christian Scientists constantly employ the Psalms of Israel as proof of their dogma. The founder of that Church in her text-book, *Science and Health*, quotes copiously from the Jewish Bible. I have even met Christian Scientists who tried to convince me of their belief by citations of passages from Jewish Scriptures.

Yet the supreme expression of the God-idea, the Psalmody, is strictly Jewish in origin. The Psalms were written *by Jews for Jews.* They represent the very inner life of Israel in the Second Commonwealth, and breathe throughout the spiritual atmosphere that characterized the Hebrews of that epoch. Moreover, the Jewish Bible fairly teems with instances of healing by Faith and Prayer.

The Prayer Book of Israel, known as the *Tefillah*, was written in the conviction that God alone is the Healer of Sickness. The doctrine of the Resurrection of the Dead is also a cardinal feature of the principal liturgy, the *Shemoneh Esreh* or Seventeen Benedictions. All in all, the Jewish writings, Biblical and Rabbinical, contain many distinct references to the Law of Divine Healing. This book contains a complete index to every important passage, and also reprints in full every passage from the Jewish Bible which reflects the truth of Jewish Science.

But the belief in Faith Cure is not merely a literary antique of Israel. In its zigzagging course, Judaism gave birth to a movement which was the historical expression of Jewish Science. Two centuries before Christian Science appeared, the Jews of Russia, Poland and Galicia initiated the Chasidic movement, which antedated and anticipated Christian Science, Theosophy, New Thought and similar cults. Chasidism which began in the Eighteenth Century spread like wildfire through central Europe, and the Wonder-Rabbi, Baal Shem Tob, or Besht became to the Chasidim what Mary Baker Eddy is to the Christian Scientists. This remarkable and unique Jewish sect will be carefully treated in Chapter Two, entitled "The Chasidic Movement." It is important to note that this movement still exists in Russia and Poland, and that Jewish Science is a living reality to millions of Jews in those countries.

My aim is to present the entire subject of Jewish Science in a clear and complete manner. In no way do

I propose to suggest the creation of a new sect in universal Israel that has been so singularly free from schisms. What is implied in Jewish Science is so thoroughly Jewish that it already occupies an important place in Jewish Theology. Nor do I mean to derogate from the medical art, which from time immemorial has been recognized in the Jewish religion as one of the *Divine Agencies* in healing the sick. The Bible itself contains many laws of hygiene, and recognizes the use of medicines. The Talmud contains accounts of rare surgical operations. The recognition of the physician is shown in the special prayer laid down in the Jewish ritual for the sick person. In his petition to God, the invalid not only prays for Divine Help, but also asks God to inspire the attending physician with wisdom that *he may heal the sufferer.* But despite its recognition of medical science, Judaism ascribes to the Supreme Being the chief potency in effecting a cure. If the physician can be dispensed with, so much the better for the individual who relies upon the power of prayer alone. At times, faith and medicine combined seem to heal a sick person and sometimes only the physician's art may be the saving power. In all cases, reliance on Divine Providence has been encouraged by the Jewish Faith, and Jewish Science is surely worth while knowing. The Chosen People who constantly proclaim their divine mission, should be the last to discourage the use of those spiritual agencies that help the body as well as the mind and heart.

Several years ago, I realized that the modern Synagogue had lost this spiritual art, and that, under the influence of radical thought which minimized Emotion and Sentiment, and exalted Reason and Logic, the average Jew of today was losing his prayerful sense. Some factor is missing in the modern synagogue, and I have concluded that it is *the art of genuine prayer in its real influence on every day life.* Once this art is restored, our places of worship will be again filled by genuine believers in the power of prayer. Our people will turn once more to "The Living God" as in the days of the Psalmists, and Prayer will be restored to its pristine place.

It is my fervent hope that this work on Jewish Science will assist in the work of spiritual renaissance. When once circulated and understood, the Jews of today will learn that their own religion offers them a complete cup of salvation. Moreover, this special compilation bearing the hallmark of Judaism will form a useful hand book of Divine Healing, for the Jew who seeks that truth, as well as for the devout and God-fearing Israelite. To the purpose of making Judaism a living reality and an ever-present help this work is dedicated, with the pious prayer that in the language of our fathers it may be "*Le Shem Shomayim*" or "In the Name of God."

CHAPTER 1

The Principle of Divine Healing

Since the days of primitive man, two distinct problems have engaged the attention of Religion. These questions have been in more or less degree the concern of all religions, whether crude or civilized. One lies in the Moral Realm; the other in the Physical. I refer to the subjects of Sin and Sickness. Sin represents the Abnormal Ethical State. Sickness corresponds to the Abnormal Bodily Condition. Sin and Sickness are neither *natural* nor *God-given.*

Since the beginning of time, mankind has sought to solve the problem of Sin. To this special moral task, Religion has dedicated itself. In its final analysis, Religion is a finite effort to attain the Divine and Infinite Perfection. Religion therefore aims, first of all, at a purely ethical purpose. In this sense, all religious customs, ceremonies, forms and symbols are only the means for the *moral* betterment of humanity. Were the world perfect, the Synagogue and the Church would inevitably lose one of their chief functions. This perfect state of human goodness is the Millennium that all religious workers and leaders are striving to effect. It is the Messianic Era when only the Right will prevail, and the Wrong be utterly eradicated.

But man is not yet perfect, and the moral struggle has gone on through the ages. At times, human nature seems little improved. Each age also presents its peculiar moral problems and at the dawn of the Twentieth Century, the present World-War has revived a host of ethical evils. War itself is an abnormal moral state, a complete contradiction of the gospel of Love which religion has always promulgated. So-called civilized nations have been guilty of cruel acts that bespeak a savage ethical code. Moral atavism characterizes the international duel, now being fought in the Old World. Evidently, in the words of the poet Tennyson, "Man has not yet lost the tiger and the ape."

The *moral* effort of Religion must still continue. The existence of the least evil is a constant stimulus to its task. Now all religions, primitive and civilized, have dealt with this paramount problem. All faiths have had the ethical implication, and whether the devotee worshipped a stick or a stone, a star or a planet, an animal or a man, he inevitably sought moral inspiration from his god or gods. Somehow, no matter how crude the religion, Morality became connected with it. This is true despite the fact that, in every pantheon of deities, there may be found a few powers of evil and malevolence. For instance, the Zoroastrian religion taught the existence of the power of good, *Ahriman*, and the power of evil, *Ahura-Mazda*, between whom there occurred a constant cosmic struggle. The Medieval people implicitly believed in an evil being who wrought all the mischief in the world. He was called either Satan or the Devil,

Lucifer or Mephistopheles. When the evil power took hold of a man, he was not responsible for his misconduct or misdeeds.

Such views, however, have not in the least detracted from the prime emphasis laid upon the moralizing power of Religion, and even in the crudest systems of faith, man has somehow stumbled on the *moral values.* Professor Jastrow in his scholarly work "The Evolution of Religion," shows conclusively that the pure ethical and spiritual principles in all religions were slowly evolved from the most primitive cults, such as Animism, Fetishism, and Ancestor Worship. The great World Religions, such as Judaism, Islam and Christianity, were the products of a religious evolution that went on for thousands of years. The light of the moral ideal somehow glimmered in the mental twilight of the race.

Now, the higher religions have constantly used all their forces as the vehicle of teaching morality. Sin, which means all moral evil, has been the target of religion's attack throughout the ages. Individuals and nations have been and still may be saved by means of Faith and Prayer. A moral evil is curable by the appeal to the *divine* or *better* sense of man. The soul of the sinner is treated by moral remedies, compounded in the laboratory of faith. The more evil in a community, the stronger the religious effort of the moral leaders or reformers. It is safe to assert that nearly every great wrong has been righted by religion. Every important moral reform has been fostered and upheld by the dynamic power of the religious element. For example, the Puritans of England with their austere faith fought the evils of their day and regarded themselves as champions of the God of Righteousness. The abolition of slavery in all parts of the civilized

3

world was largely the result of a religious movement. Today the forces of religion in the United States have combined against all existing wrong, and when evils are to be remedied, the ministers are usually the first to protest against the evils in question. All religious organizations unite in the World-War on WorldWrong.

Moreover, the best ethical thinkers have found out that Religion strengthens and intensifies morality. Witness the change in mind of Dr. Felix Adler, the founder of Ethical Culture. At the outset of his movement, Dr. Adler boldly proposed that the teaching of pure ethics was sufficient. The God-Idea was either tabooed or seldom mentioned. However, in recent years, the founder of Ethical Culture has completely veered around, and now insists on the theistic background and sanction to moral instruction. He too has come to recognize, the moral *motive-power* in the God-Conception, and the value of religious intensity, or God-Intoxication in the field of morals.

So much for the ethical side and purpose of Religion. Now, let us apply the principles we have deduced to the all absorbing problem in the physical world— Sickness or Disease. *The war on sickness has been as much the business of Religion, as of Science.* From the earliest times, men have turned to their religion for help and healing of their physical ills, just as they sought moral benefit through the same channels. The medicine-man of the Indian still acts as the medium of the tribal or tutelary god in effecting a cure. He usually employs noise-making instruments or other devices to arouse the suppliant, and works upon the sense of credulity, natural to the crude man. In some cases, magic herbs are employed. In others, written formulae, inscribed with great unction, are used to help the sufferer. Then too, all deities whom

4

man has worshipped have been constantly propitiated by the sick and the suffering. Fervent and ecstatic prayers are uttered before the image or Ikon. The Alaskan Indians today in praying for the sick perform a weird dance around the totem pole, which represents the local or tribal god. If the totem is that of the bear clan, the dancers array themselves in skins of that animal. It is safe to assert that, in all religions, primitive, ancient and modern, there exists the custom of appealing to the higher powers for aid to the sick. Religion has inevitably carried with it the idea of faith-cure or divine healing. Just as Religion has warred on Sin, so it has also fought against Sickness.

What is sickness? It is first of all an Unreal or Abnormal Condition of the Body and the Bodily Functions. Health is natural and therefore Godgiven. Sickness is ungodly or unnatural. The following theorems are accepted by both Religion and Science.

1. The body is the creation of an All-Wise and All-Good God.

2. Sickness is the violation of the laws of nature or God.

3. Health depends largely on the use of the body by the individual. Misuse or abuse of the body brings sickness and disease.

4. Worry, anxiety, and similar mental states cause physical weakness and impairment. Good Cheer, Optimism, and similar mental states promote health or well-being.

5. Faith or Religion is the highest expression of Optimism. Therefore, Religion fosters health, and fights sickness.

6. Religion in all forms has been the chief means of cultivating Cheerfulness, Optimism, and all those states that enter into the better mood.

7. The God-Idea is the very essence of all modern religions. This idea implies absolute faith in the goodness of God.

8. Judaism for thousands of years has taught the pure God-Idea.

9. Judaism has encouraged the use of Prayer and Devotion in Healing the Sick.

10. Judaism teaches Jewish Science, or the Law of Divine Healing.

Now what is the psychological factor, or agent, in all cases of faith-cure? The answer is very simple— It is the use of the power of Auto-Suggestion. The mind of man alone has the unique or peculiar function of being able to suggest to itself ideas which work themselves out in the subconscious self. This subconscious self or mind is the real mind in which man lives, moves and has his being, and by which all bodily functions are controlled and disciplined. Let us take the example of walking. To a child, walking is a painful and conscious effort. Later by gradual practice, the act of walking becomes an unconscious or subconscious process. This law holds good of all human arts and processes that require a gradual study and mastery.

The finished pianist, the trained orator, and the fine singer, attain the acme of their various arts by training of the subconscious faculties, dealing with these arts. This is an axiom of education, long since recognized.

Now all strong suggestions help in the healing process. The good physician realizes this truth, and it is a trite saying that "Confidence in the physician is half the battle of the patient." The sick man who has faith in his doctor already helps himself. At some stage of his treatment, the invalid must receive in addition to drugs or surgical relief powerful suggestions that intensify and strengthen his hope of recovery.

Then too, medicine is but a God-given agency, and in all cases of sickness, the physician can do naught else than use the divine laws and bend them to his purpose. Faith and Science are not wide apart in the treatment of sickness, but thoroughly in harmony. Now, of all suggestions that the subconscious mind can appropriate, *none is more effective than the pure idea of Faith in an All-Good God.* In the first place, the God-idea is the overarching idea of the human mind. It is the most comprehensive thought that the mind of man can take up. Moreover it carries with it the utmost emotional or driving force. It is conviction, raised to the highest degree.

In Judaism, the idea of Divine Healing has long been known. In its purest form, it is found in the Jewish Scriptures. The Bible of Israel is rich in passages teaching the healing function of God. Moreover, as will be explained in a later chapter, the Jewish Writ contains many historical incidents, vividly describing instances of divine healing. Many of the Prophets, such as Elijah, Elisha, Isaiah, and Jeremiah are represented as divine healers. Later on we shall see that a complete Jewish Science movement, known as Chasidism, arose *in the Eighteenth Century in Russia and Poland.*

The Chasidim were faith-healers in their day, and the Zaddik or mediator of the modern Chasidim still professes the curative power, derived from a higher source.

Jewish Science is not an anomaly in the Jewish faith. The Prayer Book or Tefillah of Israel contains specified prayers for divine healing. From time immemorial, it has been customary for devout Jews to offer such prayers for the sick, and to go to the Synagogue to pray for their dear ones who are suffering. One of the leading physicians of this country, an Israelite, whose name is a household word in his treatment of sickness, employs the *dual* method of Prayer and Medicine.

Faith may or may not move mountains, but it is a powerful lever in lifting the sick and despondent to the higher level of Health and Happiness. Faith does make men strong and happy. It creates new interest and enthusiasm, and teaches the value of spiritual joy as against temporal pleasure. Faith not only helps to heal, but it is an offset to *materialism.* The average Jew, like his neighbor, is often shaken by the hand of fate and fortune. When disaster overtakes him, he is usually plunged into despair and despondency. Melancholy often ensues as a result of material failure, and suicide, once unknown among the Jews, is often resorted to, as the means of solving the individual problem. Judaism still offers in its thought and ritual the *spiritual power* by which *mental unrest* may be prevented and checked. The pious Jew knows this truth only too well, and, in his supreme faith, smiles at mere worldly loss. Through his Jewish rearing, he has acquired the power which conquers Discontent, Ennui, Wanderlust, and other modern vagaries. *By his positive conviction,* he finds Health and Happiness, and drives out every thought or emotion that disturbs the body or mind. To the real Jew, Religion is still what it was to his fathers, an ever-present help in the time of trouble. It fills him *with the love of life,* with all its manifold moral and spiritual opportunities. In fact, Chayim or Life is the Ruling Passion of the Jewish soul. Life is precious and well-being desirable. For this reason, the Jewish people have been characterized by their *longevity.* The death-rate among Jewish people is much lower than that among non-Jews, and insurance experts declare that the average Jew is the very best risk. "A Long Life and a Happy One" is a maxim which sums up the greatest aspiration of a pious Israelite.

The principle of divine healing in Judaism might be further unfolded, but the reader should know by now, that Jewish Science is a living reality in the heart of Israel. The Jew who seeks this spiritual truth need not step outside of the Synagogue to find it. No alien cult is necessary to teach him the value of prayer as a means of Health and Happiness. Jewish Science contains *every important principle in the art of Divine Healing.* Christian Science and similar faiths are not needed by the true Jew who knows and loves his Religion. In Chapter Six of this work, a complete Anthology of Jewish Science may be found. In this Chapter, I have translated in full every passage from the Jewish Bible and Prayer Book that teaches Divine Healing. To this Anthology, the reader may refer in order to find special literature. He may also make use of the Jewish prayers for the sick, and put them to practical benefit. Suffice it to state that historic

Judaism has absolutely taught the principle of Faith-Cure, and that all Jewish literature, Biblical and post-Biblical, teems with references to this theme. Just as Religion in the past has fought the dual problems of Sin and Sickness, likewise Judaism through Jewish Science has combated the twofold evils. In the tents of Israel, *the spiritual truth has been taught that the ills of the flesh and the sins of the soul can be overcome by the divine power of Prayer and Good Deeds.*

CHAPTER 2

The Chasidic Movement

"Presenting in its inner motives one of the most peculiar phenomena of religious psychology in general, Chasidism should be classed among the most momentous spiritual revolutions that have influenced the social life of the Jews, particularly those of Eastern Europe."—(Jewish Encyclopedia.)

Jewish Science received *its first historical expression* in the unique movement known as Chasidism which originated in the Eighteenth Century and has continued to the present time. This unusual cult spread so rapidly that at one time it threatened to overwhelm the entire Judaism of Europe. During its growth, it obtained a hold upon practically all the Jewish masses of Poland and Russia. As stated in the quote above, it played a most important role in shaping Jewish thought and life among the Jews of the Old World.

The name Chasidism is derived from the Hebrew word, Chasid which means "A Pious Man." Chasidism therefore may be well summed up as "Intense Piety." In a manner, it resembles Christian Protestantism in that it assigns the first place in Religion not to Dogma and Ritual, but to Sentiment and Emotion. The Chasidic Movement was in the first place a distinct protest against the rigid legalism that had crept into the Jewish Faith after the Fall of the Second Temple in 70 CE. In this respect, it was but a recurrence of a phenomenon that has appeared over and over again in historic Judaism.

For two principles have constantly contended for supremacy in the spiritual life of Israel, the Law and the Spirit, Formalism and Religious Sentiment. A constant struggle has gone on between these two opposing ideas, or as the Jewish Encyclopedia expresses the thought, "The discipline of the Law was pitted against mystical and individual Mediation." The contest of these contending ideas was reflected first in the struggle between the Pharisees and the Essenes in the Second Commonwealth. The Pharisees represented the Rabbinical Law and contended for the Letter as well as the Spirit of faith. The Essenes who were the early Jewish ascetics spurned the Temple-worship and the observance of the Law. They were the first Jewish free-lances. Later, Talmudism came into conflict with the movement known as the Kabala. The Kabalists were the first pure Jewish Mystics to whom the Law alone was not a sufficient source of spiritual stimulus. Neither Essenism nor Kabalism obtained a strong hold on the masses. The ascetic view of life somehow has never appealed to the Jewish mind, and the esoteric teachings of the Kabala were beyond the ken of the plain people.

Now, the Jewish world was to witness a genuine struggle between the Law and the Spirit. Out of this conflict, emerged what we may call the Jewish Science sect known as Chasidism. During the course of the ages, the Rabbinical Law had developed into a rigid system of religion. The Study of the Law or Talmud Torah had become the Ruling Passion of the house of Israel. Talmudic learning was exalted as the chief virtue and the Practice of the Law had become the very end of life. Whatever is implied in Jewish orthodoxy, is represented in the term, *Rabbinism.* Every Jewish duty or Mitsvoh still observed by the orthodox Jew, is a part of this Rabbinical system of life. Line upon line, precept upon precept, the Rabbinical tradition had accumulated, and, at the beginning of the Eighteenth Century, Judaism had crystallized into a code of religious practice.

Now, Rabbinism was to encounter its first stumbling block in the Mystic-Messianic Movements that swept over the Jews of Russia and Poland on the threshold of the Eighteenth Century. Political and economic causes favored the spread of mystical ideas. For centuries, the Jews of Poland had enjoyed unlimited freedom and prosperity. Under the special protection of the Polish kings, Israel had grown and flourished in all parts of the Polish nation. The era of happiness did not last long for the Jewish peoples. For, at the beginning of the Eighteenth Century, there ensued a fearful period of persecution and suffering. This was mainly due to what is known as the Cossack Uprising, or the Chmielnicki Rebellion. Poland was turned from a garden spot into a veritable desert by the terrible Cossacks, who, as agents of Russia, brought about the revolution. The whole life of Polish Jewry was completely upset. The larger communities were

13

broken up and distress and poverty appeared everywhere. This period has ever since been regarded as a nightmare of Jewish suffering.

Conditions were worse in the Southwestern provinces, known as the Ukraine. These provinces were Volhymnia, Podolia and Galicia. Even before the Cossack Uprising, the Jews of the Ukraine had not enjoyed the same prosperity and opportunity as those of the northern province, known as Lithuania. In that section, the cities were larger and the educational advantages were much greater. In the principal cities, such as Wilna and Kovno, Jewish life was organized on a very large scale. Here were found the great Synagogues and Rabbinical Academies. Lithuania had become one of the strongholds of Rabbinical Orthodoxy. It is well to bear in mind the religious and economic differences between the Jews of the Ukraine and those of Lithuania.

This very difference furnished a fertile field for the growth of mystic movement. Again, under the influence of the Kabalists, the Rabbinical authorities had gradually added to Jewish life many ascetic features, such as fasting, self-torture and gloominess. "Such a combination of religious practices suitable to hermits, was not suitable to the bulk of the Jewish people." (Jewish Encyclopedia.) Even in the Northern and Lithuanian provinces, many learned and thinking Jews began to doubt the validity of the Rabbinical Law. Rabbinism was losing its strong hold over the masses as well as the free-thinking element. Skepticism coincided with the historical forces to initiate a new movement in Israel. Because of their great distress caused by the Cossack Uprising, the people were ready to turn to a new scheme of salvation that would at least offer solace for earthly suffering.

The Rock of the Law at last was about to crumble under economic and spiritual onslaught. Judaism hardened into a legal code was to be struck by the rod of another Moses that it might bring forth the living waters of faith.

This situation might be compared to that which developed a century later in Germany and the United States. About the close of the Eighteenth Century, there appeared in Berlin the towering genius of Moses Mendelsohn, the first German Jewish Reformer. In his boyhood, he was reared in the typical Rabbinical atmosphere. Until his eighteenth year, he was untouched by modern culture and life. This was practically true of all his German Jewish contemporaries. Moreover, even the German language was forbidden or unknown. The Jewish Jargon or Yiddish was the vernacular of the people. Mendelsohn secretly mastered the German language, and in his plastic mind, it became the key that unlocked the gates of the mental Ghetto into which the Jew had been forced by bias and prejudice. Mendelsohn came to Berlin where he began his task of leading his people into the broader life of Germany. Under the influence of Frederick the Great, a new and liberal spirit was fostered. The day of the Ghetto was over, and the Jew was ready to step out into the modern world. Mendelsohn first translated the Hebrew Bible into the German language, but very wisely used the Hebrew alphabet in transliterating the German words. The publication of the first German translation of the Jewish Bible created a new epoch in German Judaism. It was the first striking reform in Jewish life. Naturally it encountered the intense opposition of the orthodox or Rabbinical party. All through his lifetime, the great reformer had to fight against the powers of conservatism and traditionalism.

Later in Germany there appeared a galaxy of Jewish reformers, such as Friedlander, Zunz and Geiger. Under their influence, Reform Judaism arose as a protest against dead formalism and dry-as-dust pedantry. The reformers claimed that Judaism should be a modern and living faith, not an antiquated cult. They contended that the spirit of Judaism was more important than the letter of the Law. They also insisted that the Bible contained the living word of God which had been obscured by the thick deposit of custom and tradition. Through them, Judaism in Germany became modernized and adapted to the spirit of the times.

Later in the United States, my sainted teacher, Isaac M. Wise who had come here from Europe continued the battle of Reform. Although reared in strict orthodoxy, he soon learned on his arrival in the new land of promise that Judaism could not exist or thrive unless it was liberated from its Rabbinical interpretation. Beginning in Albany, NY, in 1849, he labored for fifty years for the living and liberal presentation of Judaism. His life and career are well known. His name has become a household word in American Israel. As a monument to his genius, there stands in Cincinnati, Ohio, the Hebrew Union College, which he founded in 1876 as an institution for educating American Rabbis in the modern spirit. This college has graduated many rabbis who have gone forth to spread the gospel of a living and liberal Judaism. Nowhere has the Jewish faith flourished more than on this continent, and this result is due to the historic effort of Isaac M. Wise in releasing the spirit of Judaism from its casement in law and ceremony.

Now in the Eighteenth Century, just as later in Germany and America, Rabbinism, officially entrenched, encountered in Russia and Poland its first protest in the Chasidic movement—which we may regard historically as the pathfinder of Reform Judaism. If later this movement degenerated, it cannot be denied that at the outset, Chasidism was inspired by a sincere and genuine effort to afford a living Jewish faith, and to improve the individual in *conduct* and *character.* To again quote the Jewish Encyclopedia, "It aimed not at dogmatic and ritual reform, but at a change in the believer. By suggestion, it created a new type of religious man, who placed emotion above ritual, and religious excitement above knowledge."

The founder of Chasidism was a Podolian Jew, Eliezer Baal Shem Tob. He was also called Besht, which is a combination of the words Baal Shem Tob. These words form a phrase which means "The Master of The Good Name." He was usually called The Master of the Name, and the idea implied is that he became the master of the *living name of God with its mystical and healing power over human ills.*

In that remarkable and classic sketch, "The Master of the Name," found in the Dreamers of the Ghetto, Israel Zangwill, the noted writer, has drawn a perfect pen-picture of the famous Wonder Rabbi—Baal Shem Tob. It is worth while reading by anyone who is interested in the Chasidic movement. We may cull certain facts from this sketch written as an autobiography by a supposed disciple of the Master of the Name. The noted Rabbi who founded Chasidism was the son of a certain Rabbi Israel who lived in

Moldavia. Shortly after his marriage, Rabbi Israel was captured by Turkish soldiers during one of their raids, and was brought to Constantinople where he was sold as a slave. Soon he found his way into the palace of the Sultan himself, who became impressed with his unusual power, for it is claimed that Israel was endowed with the gift of prophecy and fortunetelling. It is related that he obtained his freedom in the following manner. The Sultan was anxious to capture a certain city, which had defied his forces for years. He sent for the rabbi, and promised him his freedom if he could advise him successfully as to the capture of the city. The Jewish sage counseled his master to release from prison two thousand of his most dependable convicts and promise them their freedom if they would capture the city in question. The Sultan followed the suggestion, which proved wholly successful. On this account, the rabbi was granted his freedom, but the Sultan was so eager to have him in his entourage that he forced him to marry a Turkish woman and remain in the Ottoman Empire. All the while, Israel watched for an opportunity to escape, and one day succeeded in getting away from Constantinople.

Soon he rejoined his own Jewish wife and family with whom he lived happily for many years. Now the Chasidim declare that when Israel and his wife had reached their one hundredth year, a son was born to them who was the famous Baal Shem Tob, or Master of the Name. Besht was educated in the usual Jewish manner. Still, he evinced no particular talent in boyhood or early manhood. The Chasidim claim that during these years he was secretly preparing himself for his great announcement. Very little is known of his life until his thirty-eighth year. Then he began to propound his new system of faith, and also announced his power as a divine healer. His fame soon spread and followers multiplied. It is said that he cured by prayers, ecstasies and gesticulations and that he also foretold the future. Gentile and Jew flocked to him, and he became known as a miracle-worker. Baal Shem Tob appealed strongly to the masses, and became an idol of the common people. "He was characterized by simplicity and sincerity and he understood the masses. He taught that true religion does not lie in Talmudic learning, but in the love of God with faith and belief in the efficacy of prayer." (Jewish Encyclopedia). By his universal appeal and insistence on simple religion, he made Judaism a democratic faith, a religion of the people, by the people, and for the people.

Besht spent most of his life in the Podolian town of Miedzyboz. Unfortunately, he did not write a book dealing with his teachings. He usually expressed his doctrine in sayings and parables which were developed by his disciples into a formal system. Two main ideas characterized the Chasidic creed: (1) Religious Pantheism or the belief in the Divine Omnipresence; and (2) The Idea of Communion between God and man. Prayer is the best form of communion. These are the chief ideas, but other principles were expressed which surely have the modern tone. *Serve God with a cheerful and happy mind. Sadness and sorrow darken the soul.* Hence, the harm of asceticism is inferred. By constant communion, one may acquire the gift of Prophecy, and become a Zadik. This word varies with the word Chasid and is derived from the Hebrew word, which means "A Righteous Man." In the Chasidic sense, the Zadik is a mediator between God and his people.

By the usual law of historic progress, the original doctrine of the founder of Chasidism became developed into a further system—Zaddikism. This was the work of the two chief disciples of Besht, Rabbi Baer of Meseritz and Jacob Joseph Cohen of Koyno. From both places went forth many young men trained in the Chasidic cult. Meanwhile, countless Chasidic houses of worship arose to which the people turned for comfort. A special prayer book was developed and circulated. In the hour of distress, Chasidism furnished a rallying place for the sorely tried Jewish masses of the Southwestern Polish Provinces—The Ukraine.

In the Northern or Lithuanian countries where Rabbinical orthodoxy was stronger, Chasidism was naturally affected by it, and lost many of its original features. Still the cult made great inroads among the Lithuanian Jews. A new form of Chasidic faith was developed by the Lithuanian Rabbi Zalman of Liezna (1747-1812). It was known as Rational Chasidism or "Habad," derived from the first letters of the Hebrew words, *Chochmah* or Wisdom, *Binah* or Understanding, *Deah* or Knowledge. Chasidism, as stated above, was bitterly fought by the leaders of orthodoxy, when they noted the tremendous growth of the new sect. An intense struggle ensued between the opposing camps. Debates and discussions of an acrimonious nature prevailed during the entire Eighteenth Century. The doctrine of Besht, that man could be saved by Faith, was held to contradict the doctrine of Rabbinism, that man's religious value should be measured by Talmudic Learning, and Practice of the Law. The bitterest opponent of the Chasidim was Elijah Ben Solomon, who was relentless in his hostility and used all means to persecute the followers of Besht.

Chasidism attained its greatest growth in the first part of the Nineteenth Century. At that time, about half the Jews of Russia, Poland, Galicia, Romania and Hungary professed the Chasidic cult. In Russia, the sect was legalized by the government in the edict, known as "The Enactment Concerning the Jews" (1804). Elements of weakness however soon appeared. Unorganized, the Chasidim could not be held together. Then too, modern culture began to reach the Ghettoes of Poland and Russia. The younger generation turned to the movement known as "The Haskalah "or "Enlightenment." The leaders of the Haskalah began to attack the Chasidic faith as not in keeping with the spirit of the times. Other causes contributed to the weakening of Chasidism. Many of the Chasidic leaders and the Zaddikim had absolutely corrupted the pure teachings of The Master of the Name, and turned the healing art into a mere money-making scheme. Many of the leaders lived in luxury from their earnings and fees, and not a few indulged in very riotous living. Thus, Chasidism, which began as a genuine protest against Rabbinical orthodoxy, lost much of its pristine spirit. This has been the fate of many reform movements in all religions. The early reformer is inspired by pure and exalted motives. His followers later on use the new religion for impure, selfish and mercenary ends.

As an earthquake leaves its mark for centuries, likewise in religion, an upheaval has its distant and distinct effect. Chasidism is still deeply rooted in Russian and Polish Judaism, and in recent years under the stimulus of the modern healing movement in religion, it has begun to take on new life. Its historic purpose however cannot be overlooked. "In the Eighteenth Century, it was the creative force that brought into the dry bones of Rabbinism the stream of religious enthusiasm" (Jewish Encyclopedia). Nor can the purity and sincerity of Baal Shem Tob be questioned. He was a Jew of Jews, who honestly sought the welfare of his people. He was also a spiritual heir of the teachings of Moses and the Prophets. The truth of Jewish Science was found by him in the word of God, as expressed in the Jewish Scriptures. What had been taught in the Golden Age of ancient Israel, was merely taken up and repeated by him. Underlying his whole teaching was the central Jewish conviction that God alone is the King of the Universe, and the Healer of the Sick. When Jewish Science is once more recognized and restored, Baal Shem Tob will be given complete recognition in the Jewish Hall of Fame, as a true teacher in Israel, the friend of the meek and the lowly, the healer of the sick of his people. A reading of Zangwill's sketch will convince anyone that this tribute is not overdrawn. Writing as an imaginary disciple of Besht, the brilliant author concludes his masterly monograph with this exquisite thought, the facts of which are entrenched in Jewish History, and confirmed by the recognized authority on Judaism— the Jewish Encyclopedia— "But above all let the memory of the Master himself be to them a melody and a blessing: he whose life taught me to understand that the greatest man is not he who dwells in the purple, amid palaces and courtiers, hedged and guarded, and magnified by illusive pomp, but he who, talking cheerfully with his fellows in the marketplace, humble as though he were unworshipped, and poor as though he were unregarded, is divinely enkindled, so that a light shines from him whereby men recognize the visible presence of God."

CHAPTER 3

The Change of Name

One of the most curious aspects of Jewish Science is the custom, known as, *Meshanneh Hasshem* or "The Change of Name." This custom no doubt rests upon the primitive notion that the name of a person is not only an integral part of himself, but virtually *equal to his own life and being.* In ancient times, the name played a most important role, and great stress was laid upon the ceremony of giving names to individuals. The Chinese people, even today, lay so much emphasis on the name that in a lifetime a person assumes many names, just as if he were a different character under each appellation. Even in modern life the value of names is shown in the custom of giving many and varied titles to royal persons as well as nobles.

At times too, the real name is concealed, and in ancient Israel, the name of the Deity was considered so sacred that it was spoken only once a year on the Day of Atonement by the High Priest. Now the custom of changing the name of a person when sick arose in the Middle Ages among the Jews. No doubt the influence of the Kabalists or Jewish Mystics fostered the popular belief that by changing his name the sufferer could be saved from death. The notion also prevailed that in this way the Angel of Death who summons a person by name, would be baffled in his mortal purpose. The name usually adopted was *Chayyim*, which means Life. No doubt, it was believed that this name possessed vitalizing power.

The custom of changing the name of a sick person came down through the ages, and is still practiced by the Jewish people. Usually, when death seems imminent, the family of the sick person requests their rabbi to call together a special Minyan or religious assembly at the local synagogue. The regular evening or morning service is held, and at the end of the devotion, the rabbi states in a specific formula that the name of so and so is changed to such and such. A special prayer for the sick person is also offered. Such a ceremony is in vogue among those Jews who have been under the influence of the Chasidic or Jewish Science movement. Still, many devout Jews today resort to the custom in the hour of extreme sickness.

I was reared in a radical Jewish atmosphere and had never witnessed the performance of this rite, although I had known it from my Jewish studies. One day, an instance occurred which completely changed my attitude towards the question of *healing by faith*. Mr. and Mrs. A. were a couple whom I had united in marriage in Mobile, Alabama, several years ago. I was always deeply interested in their welfare, and when a daughter was born to them, I became closely attached to her. When the little child was a year old, she became very sick. Several physicians were called, and they brought their best medical skill to bear. The child grew steadily worse, and finally all hope was abandoned by the attending physicians. The mother became distracted, and naturally appealed to her family and friends for suggestions. A relative who had once witnessed the Change of Name ceremony, suggested it to the mother.

As a last hope, she requested me to come at once to perform the rite. I was compelled to turn to certain Jewish works in order to learn the proper mode of procedure, for I had never taken part in or performed the ceremony. There was no time left even to call together a Minyan at the Temple. When I arrived at the home, I found the child in a critical state. Boldly varying the usual form, I took the infant in my arms, prayed with all my strength to God, and then at the mother's advice declared the name changed from Rebecca to Ruth.

I left the house shortly after the incident, and later learnt that the child began to improve at once. Today she is three years old, and has been in fairly good health. Ever since, the parents and other friends have been firmly convinced of the efficacy of the rite. From this time too, began my own interest in Jewish Science. Let me state that at first I was altogether skeptical about the ceremony, and reluctant to perform it. But the anguish of a mother's heart could not be resisted, and I concentrated my whole being on the act of prayer for Divine Healing.

Since then I have been told of many more instances of the change of name. In some cases the rite proved successful, and, in others, the patients failed to recover.

But a large number of recoveries that I have noted, prove conclusively that Jewish Science has had its effect, and that it should recommend itself to all zealous Jews.

CHAPTER 4

Jewish Science vs. Christian Science

One of my purposes in writing this book on Jewish Science is to win back to Judaism those Jews who have been lured into the camp of Christian Science under false pretenses. Uninformed touching their own faith, these Israelites have been led to believe that Christian Science alone promulgates the truth of Divine Healing. I am broad enough to believe that in many cases the conversion to the new faith is sincere and genuine. In some instances however, it is to my mind simply a repetition of an old Jewish weakness—the desire to assimilate with the non-Jewish world.

Ever since the rise of Christianity, Jews have been converted to that religion. The Jewish Encyclopedia in the article entitled "Apostasy," contains a list of all famous Jewish apostates to the Christian faith. In the Old World, today, conversions are frequent for political or commercial preferment. Some of the most distinguished savants in Europe were born and reared in the Jewish fold. Many world-famed physicians and surgeons in Europe through sheer cowardice have embraced the dominant religion. Even Heine, that intensely Hebraic soul allowed himself to be baptized in Germany, in order to obtain certain academic advantages. As he expressed it in his characteristic way, "A few drops of water passed over my body, but did not reach my soul." The famous Lord Beaconsfield was publicly converted by his father, Isaac D' Israeli, who brought his entire family into the Established Church of England. Every Jewish community in the world has its records of defections, and personally I have known many prominent non-Jews whose ancestors had sprung from the loins of Israel.

Therefore, the conversion of Jews to Christian Science is not a new phenomenon. Nor is it to be viewed with greater alarm than the secession of many Israelites, who in the past have sold their birthright for a mess of pottage. I have admitted that in many instances the Jew, who has become a Christian Scientist, has been ingenuous in his change of faith. The psychology of the act can be easily explained. He has either suffered a grievous sickness, or seen a dear one become the victim of disease. He first has tried every school of medical thought, Allopathy, the recognized school, or the newer schools, such as Homeopathy and Osteopathy. Then, perhaps he has turned for help to New Thought, Vibration-Cure, or Animal Magnetism. One method after another was tried without success. In his final extremity, he took up the suggestion that he try the new religion of Christian Science. A drowning man clutches at a straw, and the distracted Jew begins his course in the school of Mrs. Eddy. *Science and Health* becomes his text book, and the bible of Christian Science becomes his Bible. A new heaven and earth are opened up, and the former Jew becomes an enthusiast over the discovery that *Religion is Love,* and *not Law.* He also learns that faith in God means healing of bodily ills. He does not know, or has forgotten that Judaism teaches these supreme truths of all religion. Perhaps he does not know that the idea of the love of God and man was first expressed in the Jewish Scriptures. The classic sentences which are glibly taught him by his new faith are both taken from the Pentateuch. "Thou shalt love the Lord Thy God with all thy heart, with all thy soul, and with all thy might," is taken out of the Book of Deuteronomy. The famous sentence, "Thou shalt love thy neighbor as thyself," is found in the Book of Exodus.

Then, the Jewish Neophyte is told that *Science and Health* is the first correct declaration of the principle of Divine Healing. Mary Baker Eddy naturally concedes that although she was the first to formulate the truth, it was foreshadowed in the Jewish Bible and further developed in the Christian Scriptures. She does not hesitate to use the Psalms and other parts of the Jewish Writ. In fact, her book is practically a Mosaic of Biblical quotations. Still, the main use of the word *Christian* proves that she herself wished to give a strictly Christian construction to her interpretation of Divine Healing. Therefore, the life and teachings of Jesus play a major role in *Science and Health.* According to Mrs. Eddy, the law of Healing by Faith received its highest expression in the words and acts of the Christian Messiah. In fact, the usual halo is placed on the personality of Jesus, and, in keeping with the historic attitude, Judaism is minimized that Christianity may be exalted.

In so doing, the author of *Science and Health* has merely followed in the footsteps of all Christian writers in their dealings with Jewish thought. From the time when dogmatic Christianity triumphed over the teachings of the first Christians who were merely a Jewish sect, all Christian theologians have been in the habit of depreciating the Jewish faith. They have condemned it as narrow and legalistic. Christianity was called the Religion of Love, and Judaism the Religion of Law. The Jewish Scriptures were termed the Old Testament and the Christian the New Testament. The assumption of the infinite superiority of the Christian faith over Judaism has been handed down through the ages. Mrs. Eddy does not escape the historic indictment, and every Jew in the Christian Science Church should realize that by his membership he helps to foster the century-old-fallacy. Tacitly, he approves of the custom of relegating Judaism and the Jewish Bible to a secondary place. Not enough that he has left the Oldest People of Religion, and the Oldest Religion of the People, but he has placed a stigma on the very Bible which is the fountain head of all Bibles, and all civilized religions.

While Mrs. Eddy condemned Judaism, she did not scruple to use the very best material out of the Bible which was the product of that religion. The Prophecies and Psalms of Israel are deliberately quoted, as the data of *Science and Health*. Grand larceny of thought is not yet subject to punishment. Otherwise, the author of *Science and Health* might have been indicted for this offense. How can a Jew who has become a Christian Scientist swallow such logic as this! The Old Testament was only a prelude to the New Testament. Yet it is well to quote and use the words of the Old Testament. Judaism was a religion that emphasized the law. Yet it is proper to remember the adage that sprang from Judaism, "Thou shalt love thy neighbor as thyself." In other words, Jewish literature is good enough when it is used by the Christian Scientist, but it is *not good when used by the Jew.* Judaism is a universal Religion of love, but *not when professed by Jews.* Such is the fallacious logic, employed by Mrs. Eddy and her disciples.

Now the true Jew resents all imputation cast on his faith, as found in *Science and Health.* These citations are very numerous, and will be dealt with in a separate chapter. However, we can take up certain anti-Jewish arguments. Mrs. Eddy is fond of stating that the Jewish view of the Godhead is materialistic as contrasted with the pure and spiritual conception, taught by Christian Science. Were this only the usual claim of the average Christian writer, it might be passed over, for the Jew has been accustomed to such misrepresentation of his belief. But when Jews are led into a church under this belief, it is time to protest vigorously against such thoroughly unfounded and untruthful assertions.

Far from presenting the material view of Deity, Judaism is the One Religion of Mankind that has always asserted the pure and spiritual view of the divine. Not only is this true, but Judaism has fought every effort to *materialize the God Idea.* Judaism is strictly Ethical Monotheism, pure and unadulterated. On the other hand, Christianity has always taught the idea of a god-man, or a man-god. A large portion of the Christian people still make use of images, statues, pictures, or other material representations of the divine. Christ is pictured as a flesh and blood god. The slur on Judaism would be laughable were it not so easily accepted by the gullible Jews who have accepted Christian Science.

Now, Judaism is such a simple faith that it can be summed up in the Decalogue of Sinai. These Ten Words or Commandments are the very quintessence of Judaism. The Second Commandment is absolutely the Creed of Israel touching the Godhead. This Commandment states, "Thou shalt have no other gods besides me. Thou shalt not make unto thyself any graven image, nor any likeness of anything which is in the heavens above, in the earth beneath, or in the waters under the earth. Thou shalt not bow down to them, nor serve them." The Jewish Truth may be clearly expressed in the following formula, *There is only one God who is a pure spirit not to be conceived nor represented in any material manner.* Surely Mrs. Eddy, either misinformed or prejudiced, failed to state the truth regarding Judaism.

Moreover the Jewish theory of Deity has been thoroughly realized in Jewish life and practice. The Synagogue contains no pictures, nor images of the divine. But for the Ark, containing the Scroll of the Law, and the Menorah or Sevenfold Candlestick, no vestige of anything material is found in the confines of the Jewish House of Worship. The Synagogue is as *non-material* in its suggestion of the divine, as any place of worship could possibly be.

Because of his innate prejudice against picturing the spiritual, the historic Jew developed neither art nor sculpture. In all the antiquities of Palestine, not one painting, statue nor image has been unearthed. The Jews are peculiarly spiritual in their attitude to the Godhead. Moreover, the main effort of Moses and the later Prophets of Israel was to draw the Jewish people from the pagan cults of the surrounding nations, and to educate them in Spiritual Monotheism. Witness the story of the Golden Calf. Moses rebuked Aaron and

34

the people, not only because of their worship of an animal, but because they dared to adore the Godhead through nature or a natural object.

All in all, Judaism is absolutely opposed to *materialism* whether in Religion or Philosophy. All Jewish thinkers from the days of Moses have stood for the broadest conception of Divinity. In fact, Jewish philosophy is so very spiritual that it refuses to ascribe even names or attributes to the Godhead. All limitation of the Deity by terms or epithets are proscribed by the best Jewish minds. Take for example the philosophic work "The Guide of the Perplexed," written by Moses Maimonides in the Twelfth Century. The main thesis of this book is that the conception of the *infinity of God precludes all finite limitations.* Surely, this is Monotheism, attenuated and spiritualized.

So much for the creedal side of this subject. Now let us examine the validity of Christian Science in its appeal to the Jew as a healing process. Here again we detect a case of rank injustice. Judaism was *the first religion that taught the curative power of genuine faith.* This idea has been carefully worked out in the First Chapter of this book, entitled "The Principle of Divine Healing."

Also in the Chapter on the "Chasidic Movement," the reader has learnt that in Judaism there exists a pure Jewish Science cult. For complete data, this volume contains an Anthology in which may be found in full every passage from the Jewish Bible and Prayer Book that in the remotest manner teaches the principle of Divine Healing. If the Jew who has become a Christian Scientist is not convinced by this array of facts, then he is not open to any conviction. *No Jew need to become a Christian Scientist in order to find*

35

the Law of Healing by Prayer. Christian Science offers
absolutely nothing new to the Jewish Mind. It is
simply Judaism, veneered with Christology or the
belief in the divinity of Jesus. In order to counteract
the influence of Christian Science, Jewish Science
should be cultivated in the Synagogue. I have done
this in my own congregation with the result that there
is not a single Jew in my community who affiliates with
Christian Science. Whenever there has been such a
tendency, I have sympathetically approached the
person who is tempted to take up the new faith, and
shown him the folly of leaving his own religion to seek
a truth which has been offered him in Judaism for
centuries. In every case, I am happy to state that I
succeeded in keeping the faltering person in the
Jewish fold.

Persecution has not been the rule of Israel, and the
people who have suffered more than any other for their
belief should be the last to crusade against Jews who
have been drawn into Christian Science. Judaism has
never been a proselytizing nor a persecuting religion.
We ought to deal gently with our coreligionists who
have been tempted by the new cult, and win them
back to their older faith by showing that Judaism
teaches in a pure and simple way the law of divine
healing.

There is a soul of goodness in things evil, and in a
way Christian Science has benefited Judaism. I have
often heard it said by Jews who dabbled in Christian
Science that it has made them better Jews. By this,
they meant that they had somehow lost their Jewish
enthusiasm, and when they began to study Christian
Science, they found that it had merely taken a Jewish
truth, and redressed it in a new garb. Since Christian
Science has made some inroads into the Jewish ranks,

the Jewish leaders of today have been forced to study the situation, to find some method of combating this tendency. There has been considerable heart-searching in Israel, and the Central Conference of American Rabbis has begun to take up the problem. For this reason, I believe it is well to educate the growing generation in the true Jewish doctrine, and to teach not only the abstract, but the *practical* value of faith. It is my opinion, that this work on Jewish Science answers a genuine demand, and that it offers a spiritual weapon by which Christian Science may be fought from the Jewish standpoint.

Let the Synagogue offer to the Jew the original truth regarding Divine Healing and Judaism will reclaim all of its former devotees, especially those who have drifted into the Christian Science Church. Let the saving truth of the Jewish faith be openly stated so that the modern Jew may find in his own prayers and ritual the spiritual principle which is so strongly emphasized in the newer cults. In other words, Jewish Science should be directly taught to the Jews of today, and the rising generation especially should be carefully instructed in the pure and simple doctrine of divine help and healing, as it is contained in Jewish Tradition and Literature. Let Jewish Science be taught to Jews so that Christian Science may be counteracted in its insidious effort to lead Jewish people away from the real Jewish truth. It is to be hoped that this book will serve as an instrument of Jewish information and enlightenment. Intended primarily for the Israelite who seeks the principle of Divine Healing, it should serve as a special hand book for all classes of Jews. *For Jewish Science is not of today nor of yesterday, but it is an eternal principle of the Jewish soul.* It is part and parcel of the Godconsciousness which forms the very essence of the Jewish faith. Merely to teach the Divine unity and existence is not sufficient, but the secondary and important truth of Jewish Science should be constantly emphasized, viz: *that God alone is the Healer of the sick of His people, Israel.*

CHAPTER 5

A Refutal of Anti-Jewish References
in *Science and Health*

In this Chapter, I propose to answer and refute many anti-Jewish statements, contained in *Science and Health*, written by Mary Baker Eddy. As stated in the previous chapter, the author evinces a strange bias towards Judaism and Jewish Literature. Either through ignorance or prejudice, she has glibly published in her book sentences and passages which reveal a woeful misunderstanding of the true spirit of the Jewish Faith. All such statements are taken for granted by her followers, and Jews who have become Christian Scientists are completely misinformed as to their former religion. Elsewhere, I have answered the general charge of Mrs. Eddy, that Judaism teaches a material view of the God-head, and that the principle of Divine Healing is not taught by the Jewish Faith. Now I will take up in detail every passage in *Science and Health* in which Mrs. Eddy attacks Judaism, and in so doing will follow her book from beginning to end.

(1) On page 23, *Science and Health* makes the following statement: "Rabbinical lore said, 'He that taketh one doctrine firm in faith, has the Holy Ghost dwelling in him.' This preaching receives a strong rebuke in the Scripture, 'Faith without works is dead.' Faith, if it be mere belief, is as a pendulum swaying between something and nothing, having no fixity."

In the first place, the quotation from the rabbis is mistranslated. In the Talmud, this statement is made which Mrs. Eddy has perverted: "He that taketh one doctrine in the spirit, has the holy spirit dwelling in him." The phrase "The Holy Ghost," is not Jewish. Moreover, the author of this statement meant to teach exactly the opposite of that which Mrs. Eddy has stated. He really attacked Dogmatism, and declared that Doctrines or Dogmas should be accepted and realized in the spirit which means the Deed. Moreover, Judaism has never emphasized mere faith in creed or doctrine. If anything, Judaism has laid stress on religious acts, ceremonies, and moral actions. The New Testament constantly attacks the Old Testament because it teaches the value of works or deeds. In fact, Christianity arose as a protest against the overpractical interpretation of religion by the Pharisees. In one sentence, Mrs. Eddy attacks Judaism because it teaches faith with works, and in this passage, she has taken an isolated statement in the Talmud, mistranslated it, and declared that Judaism teaches faith without works. As stated above, Judaism emphasizes Deed and not Creed, and the inner or spiritual truth in its practical effect, rather than a mere dogma or doctrine.

(2) On page 30, *Science and Health* contains the following statement: "Rabbi and priest taught the Mosaic Law which said, 'an eye for an eye,' and

'Whoso sheddeth man's blood, by man shall his blood be shed.' Not so did Jesus the new executor for God, present the divine law of Love, which blesses even those that curse it."

First of all, the rabbis and priests did not teach the Mosaic Law which said, "An eye for an eye, etc." The Jewish Law of punishment was gradually developed in the Second Commonwealth by the Synhedrion or Sanhedrion—the Great Jewish Assemblage which laid down all the laws for the Jews between the Babylonian exile and the Fall of the Second Temple in 70 CE. The Jewish authorities of that epoch naturally believed in and enforced the law against crime, just as all civilized nations do today. Capital punishment still exists in almost all modern nations,[1] and each crime is adequately punished. Without proper enforcement of the law, society could not exist.

Now, let me explain the Mosaic law, "An eye for an eye, etc." This statement is found in Exodus, Chapter 21:24. In this sentence, Moses laid down the principle still known in law as "Lex Talionis" or "The Law of Retaliation." Every Bible student knows this. Moreover, this law was never meant nor taken literally by Jewish people. It would be a physical impossibility to exact such ridiculous punishment, as taking an eye from a man who had destroyed the eye of another. Jesus, in the New Testament is credited with some very cruel statements. For example, take the following passage from Matthew, Chapter 10, verses 34, 36: "Think not that I came to send peace on the earth. I came not to send peace, but a sword. I came to set a

---

[1] *Editor's Note:* The author's statement regarding capital punishment was written in 1916. In January 2011, only 58 countries retain capital punishment in both law and practice.

man against his father, the daughter against her mother, and the daughter-in-law against her mother-in-law, and a man's foes shall be they of his own household." Now, if this statement is taken literally, Jesus should be considered in a very harsh light. But every student of the Bible knows that a prophet or leader should be judged by his noblest expression, and not by ignoble thoughts which often are credited to him. Now, Moses did not mean to teach literally the doctrine of "An eye for an eye." On the other hand, he and not Jesus presented for the first time "The Divine Law of Love." Even the New Testament admits this absolute fact. Let me quote from the Gospel of Matthew, Chapter 22, verses 35-40: "And one of them, a lawyer, asked him a question trying him. Teacher, which is the great commandment in the Law? And he said unto him, THOU SHALT LOVE THE LORD THY GOD, WITH ALL THY HEART, WITH ALL THY SOUL, AND WITH ALL THY MIGHT (taken from a verse spoken by Moses in Deut. 6:5.) This is the great and first commandment, and a second like unto it is this, THOU SHALT LOVE THY NEIGHBOR AS THYSELF (taken from a verse spoken by Moses in Lev. 19:18.) On these two commandments, hang the whole Law and the Prophets."

(3) On page 30, *Science and Health* contains the following statement: "As the individual ideal of Truth, Christ Jesus came to rebuke the rabbinical error and all sin, sickness and death—to point out the way of Truth and Life. This ideal was demonstrated throughout the whole earthly career of Jesus, showing the difference between the offspring of Soul and of material sense of Truth and of error."

Mrs. Eddy continues to harp on the phrase, "Rabbinical error." The entire term is unhistorical and illogical. The rabbis of Israel have held *various opinions* regarding Religion, and these views are scattered through a period of *two thousand years or more.* If the author had in mind the rabbis and Jewish teachers of the time of Jesus, she was very much mistaken in her estimate of their spiritual worth. Evidently, Jesus did not come to rebuke rabbinical error, but rather to confirm the doctrine of the rabbis and Jews of his day. The following passage from the Gospel of Matthew is proof sufficient. In the famous Sermon on the Mount, Jesus paid the following tribute to Judaism: "Think not that I came to destroy the law of the Prophets. I came *not to destroy but to fulfill,* for verily I say unto you, Till heaven and earth pass away, one jot or one tittle shall in no wise pass away from the law, till all things be accomplished. Whosoever therefore shall break one of the least commandments, and shall teach men so, shall be called least in the kingdom of heaven. But whosoever shall do and teach them, he shall be called great in the kingdom of heaven. For I say unto you, that except your righteousness shall exceed the righteousness of the scribes and Pharisees, ye shall in no wise enter the kingdom of heaven."

(4) *Science and Health* on page 42 makes the following statement: "Jesus' life proved, divinely and scientifically, that God is love, whereas priest and rabbi affirmed God to be a mighty potentate, who loves and hates. The Jewish theology gave no hint of the unchanging love of God."

This statement is completely unfounded. *Judaism absolutely teaches that God is Love.* The principle of divine love is constantly expressed in the Jewish

Scriptures. Let me quote only a few texts describing God as the God of love:

"The Lord did not set his *love* upon you nor choose you because you were more in number than any people, for ye were the fewest of all people. But because the Lord *loved* you, and because he would keep the oath which he swore unto your fathers, hath the Lord brought you out with a mighty hand, out of the house of bondsman, from the hand of Pharaoh, King of Egypt." (Deut. 7:8.)

"In all their affliction he was afflicted, and the angel of his presence saved them. In His Love, and in His pity He redeemed them; and He bare them, and carried them all the days of old." (Isaiah 63:9.)

"The Lord Thy God in the midst of thee is mighty; He will save, and will rejoice over thee with joy. He will rest in His Love, He will joy over thee with singing." (Zeph. 3:17.)

"O Lord! by these things men live, and in all these things is the life of my spirit, so wilt thou save me and make me to live. Behold for peace I had great bitterness. But Thou hast in Love delivered my soul from the pit of corruption, for Thou hast cast all my sins behind Thy back." (Isaiah 38:16-17.)

"Wherefore it shall come to pass, if ye hearken to these judgments, and keep and do them, that the Lord Thy God shall keep the covenant and the mercy which he sware unto thy fathers. And He will love thee, and bless thee and multiply thee." (Deut. 7:12-13.)

There are many similar passages in Jewish Writ, but these excerpts should convince the most prejudiced reader, that Judaism teaches a God of Love and Forgiveness. In fact, Judaism has laid more stress on penitence and atonement, than any other faith. Judaism does not teach that man is perfect. Nor does it set up the model of a perfect man. One of the holiest days in the Jewish Religion is Yom Kippur, or the Day of Atonement, on which an entire day is spent by the devout Jew in prayer and penitence. Judaism teaches that God punishes or "hates" those who do evil. The same common-sense doctrine is found in all religions and has become the basis of the criminal law of all civilized nations. Whenever the Jewish Bible states that *God hates,* the meaning is simply that there is judgment for those who transgress the laws of God.

Judaism presents the well rounded idea of a God of Justice and of Love, who punishes and rewards, who exacts judgment, but also forgives the sincerely repentant. In fact, the highest and purest conception of a God of Love was taught by a Jewish Prophet— Hosea. His Prophecy of fourteen chapters may be found in the Sacred Canon, and it is worth while reading as a perfect classic of literary expression. Hosea taught that God is a God of Love, who would forgive the sins of Israel, and take them again into His favor. Let me in conclusion quote from the last chapter of Hosea, a passage that is the finest utterance in the entire Bible, touching the God of Love:

"I (God) will heal their backsliding. I will love them freely, for mine anger is turned away from them. I will be as the dew unto Israel; he shall grow as a lily, and cast forth his roots as Lebanon. They that dwell under His shadow shall return. They shall revive as the corn and grow as the vine. The scent thereof shall be as the wine of Lebanon." (Hosea 14:4-7.)

Let me also cite the universal note sounded by the Prophet Jonah. Sent to condemn the entire city of Nineveh for its sin, Jonah, according to the narrative, seemed to delight in his judicial mission. The Bible relates that he went outside of the city and built himself a booth, and sat there to see what would become of the city. Then God caused a gourd to grow as protection to the prophet. The next day He sent a worm which destroyed the gourd. When the sun beat upon the head of Jonah, he felt faint, and prayed for death. Then the Jewish Bible teaches the broad lesson of humanity and divine forgiveness in the following verses:

"And God said to Jonah, doest thou well to be angry for the gourd. And he said I do well to be angry, even unto death. Then said the Lord, Thou hast had pity on the gourd for which thou didst not labor, neither madest it to grow, which came up in the night and perished in the night, And should I not spare Nineveh, that great city, wherein are more than six score thousand persons that cannot discern between their right hand and their left hand, and also much cattle?" (Jonah 4:9-11.)

(5) Chapter Four of *Science and Health* is entitled, "Christian Science vs. Spiritualism." The author does not hesitate to quote a Jewish Prophet, Isaiah, at the beginning of this Chapter. The following sentence is cited completely from Isaiah 19:3: "And when they shall say unto you Seek unto them that hath familiar spirits, And unto wizards that peep and that mutter

Should not a people seek unto their God." I merely cite this passage from *Science and Health* to show the inconsistency of its author. In one breath, she absolutely condemns the Jewish Bible and Judaism. Yet, as a perfect paradox, she does not hesitate to use the Jewish Scriptures as proof of a particular opinion or as a dogma of Christian Science. *Science and Health* is marred throughout by this illogical inconsistency.

(6) On page 94, *Science and Health* contains the following statement: "Jesus taught but one God, one Spirit, who makes man in the image and likeness of Himself—of Spirit not of matter. Man reflects infinite Truth, Life, and Love."

The Jewish Scriptures were the first to teach that God is a Spirit, and that He made man in His image. Therefore Moses, and not Jesus taught, "One God, One Spirit who makes man in the Image and Likeness of Himself."

This is the supreme truth of Judaism, and it is taught in the First Chapter of the Hebrew Bible, in the Book of Genesis. In fact, the entire first Chapter of Genesis is merely an account of the Creation of the World and Man by the Divine Power. This is the gist of the Story of the Creation, as it is related in Genesis. Judaism has never veered in the least from the position, assumed by Moses in the opening chapter of the Jewish Bible. In other words, Judaism has taught from the very beginning of its history spiritual and ethical Monotheism. The author of *Science and Health* has taken unlimited license in the treatment of the Jewish Bible, and absolutely misstated the very primary facts contained in the Bible.

It might be well to quote the exact sentences in the book of Genesis which completely sum up and represent the Jewish Creed.

"And God said, Let us make man in our image, after our likeness and let him have dominion over the fish of the sea, over the fowl of the air, over the cattle, over the earth, and over every creeping thing that creepeth upon the earth. So God created man in his own image, in the image of God created he him, male and female, created He them."

(7) On page 109 of *Science and Health*, the following statement occurs: "The revelation of Truth in the understanding came to me gradually and apparently through Divine power. When a new spiritual idea is borne to earth, the Prophetic Scripture of Isaiah is renewedly fulfilled, 'Unto us a child is born—and his name shall be called Wonderful.'" The author of this illuminating statement again pays a high tribute to Jewish thought, for she does not hesitate to quote a Jewish Prophet in reference to her own discovery of spiritual truth. The passage in question is one of the typical Messianic passages found in the Jewish Bible. Ever since the rise of Christianity and the appearance of the New Testament, all such passages have been interpreted as referring to the Christian Messiah. As a matter of fact, not one of them can be so taken, and in recent years, Biblical scholars—themselves Christian—have given up the Christological treatment of all the Messianic Prophecies in the Jewish Scriptures. In fact, each passage can be historically referred to a Jewish king or leader, living in the age in which the passage was written.

(8) *Science and Health* contains this remarkable statement on page 110: "In following these leadings of scientific revelations, the Bible was my only text book. The Scriptures were illumined; reason and revelation were reconciled, and afterwards the truth of Christian Science was demonstrated."

What Bible did the founder of Christian Science have in mind? If she meant the Jewish as well as the Christian Bible, she surely has shown a dual attitude towards the former. The pages of her work are filled with many anti-Jewish statements, and her bias to Judaism is clearly revealed. Now, the author admits that the Bible was her only textbook. In other words, she praises that which she condemns, and condemns that which she praises. This is inconsistency in the highest degree.

(9) On page 133 *Science and Health* contains the following statement: "In Egypt, it was mind that saved the Israelites from belief in the plagues. In the wilderness, streams flowed from the rock, and manna fell from the sky. In national prosperity, miracles attended the successes of the Hebrews; but when they departed from the true idea, their demoralization began. Even in captivity among foreign nations, the divine Principle wrought wonders for the people of God in the fiery furnace, and in kings' palaces."

This statement requires no answer, for in an unguarded moment the author of *Science and Health* admits the truth regarding Judaism and the Jews. I cite this passage as a typical example of her inconsistency in dealing with Jewish thought and history. No higher tribute to the spiritual conception of the ancient Jew could be given than this. It is another proof that Jewish Science is an all-sufficient belief for the Jewish people.

(10) On the very same page, *Science and Health* makes the following statement, which is the absolute contradiction of her previous statement: "Judaism was the antithesis of Christianity because Judaism engendered the limited form of a national or tribal religion. It was a finite and material system, carried out in special theories concerning God, man, sanitary methods, and a religious cultus."

In the early days, the Jews, like all peoples, had a national or tribal religion, but Moses, the Prophets, and all Jewish leaders have for thousands of years taught an absolutely universal religion. The finest expressions of universal faith are found in the Jewish Scriptures. Let me cite one magnificent passage from the Prophet Malachi: "Have we not all one Father? Hast not one God created us all?" (Malachi 2:10.) Let me also mention the book of Ruth which is one of the purest expressions of the *universality* of Judaism. I might multiply citations from the Jewish Bible, but it is not necessary. Let me also state that Judaism has never been an exclusive religion. In all times, the Jewish religion has received new accessions from non-Jews. Under the strictest orthodox code, a Gentile may be received into the Jewish faith, and today under the influence of Reform Judaism, the doors have been thrown wide open to all non-Jews, who are willing to subscribe to the chief tenets, and especially the main principle— the belief in the One and Universal God. This should be a complete answer to the groundless charge that Judaism is a *narrow* and *national* Religion.

(11) On page 135, *Science and Health* makes the following statement: "The same power which heals sin heals also sickness. This is 'The beauty of Holiness' that when truth heals the sick, it casts out evil, and

when truth casts out the evil called disease, it heals the sick."

The author of *Science and Health* somehow could not get away from pure Jewish thought as it is expressed in the Jewish Writ. Let us take the first sentence. This is absolutely the principle of Jewish Science which declares that the power of God can heal Sin and Sickness. Mrs. Eddy even quotes the classic Jewish expression, "The Beauty of Holiness," which she excerpted from the following verse in the Psalms: "Worship the Lord in the beauty of Holiness."

(12) On page 139, the following statement is found: "From beginning to end, the Scriptures are full of accounts of the triumph of Spirit, Mind, over matter. Moses proved the power of Mind by what men call Miracles; so did Joshua, Elijah, and Elisha."

This statement explains itself. It is another proof of the inconsistent attitude of the author. In this passage, she absolutely admits that the law of divine healing was known and practiced by Moses and his successors. If Moses knew this truth, he certainly preceded Jesus by a period of twelve hundred years. Since he antedated Jesus, he must be regarded as the pathfinder in the demonstration of the law of divine healing.

(13) Let me quote, without comment, the following passage, found on page 190: "The Hebrew bard, swayed by mortal thoughts, thus swept his lyre with saddening strains on human existence.

"As for man, his days are as grass:
As a flower of the field, so he flourisheth.
For the wind passeth over it, and it is gone;
And the place thereof shall know it no more."

When hope rose higher in the human heart, he sang:

> "As for me, I will behold Thy face in righteousness
> I shall be satisfied, when I wake, with Thy
>   likeness.
> For with Thee is the fountain of life;
> In Thy light shall we see light."

(14) On page 226, the following statement is made: "The lame, the deaf, the dumb, the blind, the sick, the sensual, the sinner, I wished to save from the slavery of their own beliefs, and from the educational systems of the Pharaohs, who today as of yore hold the children of Israel in bondage."

This is another instance of the anti-Jewish bias and prejudice of the author. In other passages as we have seen, she admits that Moses took the Israelites out of the land of Egypt, which means Materialism and by the power of God, brought them into the land of Canaan, which signifies the Spiritual Life. The Jews have never been and are not today under the sway of materialistic ideas concerning the Godhead. They are not held in the bondage of superstition and supernatural belief. Judaism teaches the existence of *a pure Divine Spirit,* and upholds only *Spiritual ideas.*

(15) Let me cite for the benefit of Jew and Christian alike the following striking passage from *Science and Health.* In this passage, the author condemns the idea of the Trinity, and quotes the immortal Jewish phrase, "Hear O, Israel, the Lord our God, the Lord is One."

"The theory of three persons in one God (that is, a personal trinity, or Tri-unity), suggests polytheism, rather than the one ever present I Am, "Hear O, Israel, the Lord our God, the Lord is One."

(16) Let me continue the statement in *Science and Health*, which is another tribute to the Jewish conception of God.

"The everlasting I Am, is not bounded nor compressed within the narrow limits of physical humanity, nor can He be understood aright through mortal concepts. The precise form of God, must be of small importance, .in comparison with the sublime question, what is Infinite Mind or Divine Love? Who is it that demands our obedience? He who in the language of Scriptures "Doeth according to His will in the army of heaven, and none can stay his hand or say unto him, What doeth Thou?"

(17) On page 308, the author makes this statement: "The soul-inspired patriarchs heard the voice of Truth, and talked with God as consciously as man talks with man." Then the author uses the story of Jacob's wrestling with the angel, as a symbol of the struggle of man against error. On the following page, she sums up the struggle of Jacob as follows: "The result of Jacob's struggle thus appeared. He had conquered material error with the understanding of Spirit and of Spiritual Power. This changed the man. He was no longer called Jacob but Israel—A Prince of God or a soldier of God, who had fought a good fight."

I cite this passage as another tribute by the author to Judaism. Now, it is admitted that the Patriarchs possessed spiritual power. Let Jews who have become Christian Scientists take note of this fact.

(18) Let me again quote, without comment, the passage on page 320 in which the author continues to pay tribute to the Jewish Scriptures.

"The one important interpretation of the Scripture is the Spiritual. For example, the text, 'In my flesh shall I see God,' gives the profound idea of the Divine

Power to heal the ills of the flesh and encourages mortals to hope in Him who healeth all our diseases; whereas this passage is continually quoted as if Job intended to declare that even if disease and worms destroy his body, yet in the latter days he should stand in celestial perfection before Elohim, still clad in material flesh—an interpretation which is just the opposite of the true, as may be seen by studying the Book of Job."

(19) On page 350, the author again writes in an anti-Jewish Spirit: "In Jewish worship, the Word was materially explained, and the Spiritual sense was scarcely perceived. The Religion which sprang from half-hidden Israelitish history, was pedantic and void of healing power."

This attack on Judaism can be best answered by the author herself, who in many passages has declared that Judaism taught the spiritual truth through Jewish Scriptures. Here we note again the usual inconsistency. On the same page, a similar expression is found. This statement can also be answered by other passages in the volume.

"The Israelites centered their thoughts on the material in their attempted worship of the Spiritual. To them matter was substance, and spirit was shadow. They thought to worship spirit from a material standpoint, but this was impossible."

(20) Let me now take up the question of the Creed of Christian Science. The founder of that faith and her followers since have constantly declared that Christian Science teaches nothing which a Jew cannot accept. This is not true, as I have shown in the preceding passages. Mary Baker Eddy, as proven by her own work, was filled with anti-Jewish prejudice, and no self-respecting Jew can accept a religion whose bible

contains so many false and unfounded statements regarding Judaism. Now, as final proof that Christian Science cannot be accepted by a true Jew, or, in fact, by any real monotheist, let me publish in full the creed of Christian Science as found on page 497:

(1) "As adherents of truth, we take the inspired word of the Bible as our sufficient guide to eternal life."

Comment. The author no doubt had in mind the entire Bible—Jewish and Christian. If she accepted the Jewish Bible as inspired, she surely stultified herself, for every anti-Jewish reference in *Science and Health* is based upon her reading and interpretation of the self-same Jewish Bible. This very inconsistency should deter any Jew from taking *Science and Health* as a logical or authoritative book. An author should be consistent, and free from bias. The author of *Science and Health* constantly contradicts herself.

(2) "We acknowledge and adore one Supreme and Infinite God. We acknowledge His Son, one Christ; the Holy Ghost or divine comforter; and man in God's image and likeness."

Comment. This article of the Christian Science creed cannot be accepted by the Jew, because it unmistakably teaches the divinity of Jesus. The author claimed that the word Christ represents only a principle, but nowhere does she explain the phrase, "His Son." Christian Science no matter how it disguises itself, is trinitarian Christianity, and surely no Jew can accept a creed which in the least wise recognizes the divine superiority of Jesus. Judaism has never deified a man. Even Moses has never been regarded by the Jews as *a divine person,* but has always been called Moses our teacher. He has never been worshipped, prayed to, nor is even the place of his burial known, for fear it might become a place of worship. To paraphrase Article 2, we Jews might state the Jewish Creed as follows: "We acknowledge and adore One Supreme and Infinite God, and recognize man as created in the image and likeness of God."

(3) "We acknowledge God's forgiveness of sin in the destruction of sin and the spiritual understanding that casts out evil as unreal. But the belief in sin is punished so long as the belief lasts."

Comment. This is the only article of the Christian Science Creed that is at all Jewish. Judaism thousands of years ago taught that God forgives the sinner, if he but truly repents. Judaism recognizes the existence of sin, but teaches that sin or evil is not godlike, and can be overcome by prayer and good works. Sin is not natural, but it does exist. Otherwise, the world would be perfect. Judaism teaches a simple doctrine of Atonement. The emphasis is placed upon man, not God. "The sinner can make himself at One with his Maker, by casting his sinful past into the sea, to begin a new life of virtue, goodness and rectitude." (Kohler's Guide for Instruction in Judaism.)

(4) "We acknowledge Jesus' atonement as the evidence of divine, efficacious love, unfolding man's unity with God, through Christ Jesus, the Wayshower, and we acknowledge man is saved through Christ, through Truth, Life and Love as demonstrated by the Galilean Prophet in healing the sick and overcoming sin and death."

Comment. This entire article of the Christian Science Creed is repugnant to the Jewish belief. Judaism teaches that *no being* nor *mediator* is necessary to work atonement for man's sin. In true penitence, the Jew turns to God alone for divine pardon and forgiveness, after he himself has tried to atone for his own sin. In this article, Jesus is represented in an ambiguous way. He is regarded both as an individual and as a principle. In either sense, the author of *Science and Health* contradicts herself as stated in Article 2. "We acknowledge and adore One Supreme and Infinite God." Nothing further need be said.

(5) "We acknowledge that the crucifixion of Jesus and his resurrection served to uplift faith to understand eternal Life, even the allness of Soul, Spirit, and the nothingness of matter."

Comment. No true Jew can subscribe to this article, for as stated above, faith in a spiritual God is not taught to the Jew by the life and history of any individual. Judaism teaches the pure idea of a Godhead, independent of any man. Moses and the Prophets merely taught this idea to the Jewish people, but in no way was this belief based upon their life or work. Then, too, the Jew has been persecuted through the ages, because of the teaching of the crucifixion of Jesus, which, it is alleged, his ancestors brought about. As long as the Christian account of the crucifixion and resurrection of Jesus is taught, the Jew cannot in any way subscribe to the acceptance of this dogma, or its interpretation in *Science and Health.*

(6) "And we solemnly promise to watch, and pray for that mind to be in us which was also in Christ Jesus; to do unto others as we would have them do unto us; and to be merciful, just and pure."

Comment. This article also cannot be accepted by the real Jew for the same reasons as stated above. The spiritual truth of life is taught the Jew only through his belief in the Divine being, and not through the life of any individual. To the Jew, truth is impersonal, and the truth of God's existence is not taken in a *personal or material sense.*

Now, at. the conclusion of this Chapter, let me briefly state the creed of Judaism, or Jewish Science, as contrasted with the creed of Christian Science. (See Guide for Instruction in Judaism by Rev. Dr. K. Kohler. This is a standard Jewish work.)

(1) "We believe that there is One God, an only Being, Eternal, Spiritual and Most Holy, Who created heaven and earth, and ruleth the world with perfect wisdom, with infinite justice, and everlasting love. He is our God, and there is none besides Him. Him we are bidden to love with all our heart, all our soul, and all our might; exclaiming: 'Hear, O Israel, the Lord our God, the Lord is One.'"

(2) We believe that all men are children of God, endowed with a divine spirit, destined to share in eternal happiness by following His ways of righteousness."

(3) "We also believe that Israel, having been the first to recognize God, hath received a special revelation of His will, with the mission of being His chosen Priest among the nations, to lead them to truth and salvation."

(4) "We also believe that God ruleth and judgeth all men and nations in righteousness and love. By rewards and punishments, by joys and sufferings, he educateth and leadeth them to ever higher aims, until at last they shall arrive at the end of all time, when truth, justice, and peace shall unite mankind in the life of divine love, and eternal salvation, and God will be King and Father of all."

CHAPTER 6

A Complete Anthology of Jewish Science

ABIMELECH AND HIS HOUSE HEALED BY GOD

And Abraham journeyed from thence toward the land of the South, and dwelt between Kadesh and Shur; and he sojourned in Gerar.

And Abraham said of Sarah his wife, She is my sister: and Abimelech king of Gerar sent, and took Sarah. But God came to Abimelech in a dream of the night, and said to him, Behold, thou art but a dead man, because of the woman whom thou hast taken; for she is a man's wife. Now Abimelech had not come near her; and he said, Lord, wilt thou slay even a righteous nation? Said he not himself unto me, She is my sister? and she, even she herself said, He is my brother: in the integrity of my heart and the innocence of my hands have I done this. And God said unto him in the dream, Yea, I know that in the integrity of thy heart thou hast done this, and I also withheld thee from sinning against me: therefore suffered I thee not to touch her. Now therefore restore the man's wife; for he is a prophet, and he shall pray for thee, and thou shalt live: and if thou restore her not, know thou that thou shalt surely die, thou, and all that are thine.

And Abimelech rose early in the morning, and called all his servants, and told all these things in their ears: and the men were sore afraid. Then Abimelech called Abraham, and said unto him, What hast thou done unto us? and wherein have I sinned against thee, that thou hast brought on me and on my kingdom a great sin? Thou hast done deeds unto me that ought not to be done. And Abimelech said unto Abraham, What sawest thou, that thou hast done this thing? And Abraham said, Because I thought, Surely the fear of God is not in this place: and they will slay me for my wife's sake. And moreover she is indeed my sister, the daughter of my father, but not the daughter of my mother: and she became my wife. And it came to pass, when God caused me to wander from my father's house, that I said unto her, This is thy kindness which thou shalt show unto me: at every place whither we shall come, say of me, He is my brother. And Abimelech took sheep and oxen, and men-servants and womenservants, and gave them unto Abraham, and restored him Sarah his wife. And Abimelech said, Behold, my land is before thee: dwell where it pleaseth thee. And unto Sarah he said, Behold, I have given thy brother a thousand pieces of silver; behold, it is for thee a covering of the eyes to all that are with thee: and in respect of all thou are righted. And Abraham prayed unto God: and God *healed* Abimelech, and his wife, and his maid-servants: and they bare children. For the Lord had made barren the entire house of Abimelech because of Sarah, the wife of Abraham. (Genesis, Chapter 20.)

DIVINE HEALING, AS A RESULT OF KEEPING
THE COMMANDMENTS OF GOD

And Moses led Israel onward from the Red Sea,
and they went out into the wilderness of Shur; and they
went three days in the wilderness, and found no water.
And when they came to Marah, they could not drink of
the waters of Marah, for they were bitter: therefore the
name of it was called Marah.   And the people
murmured against Moses, saying, What shall we
drink?   And he cried unto the Lord, and the Lord
showed him a tree, and he cast it into the waters, and
the waters were made sweet.   There he made for them
a statute and an ordinance and there he proved them;
and he said, If thou wilt diligently hearken to the voice
of the Lord, thy God, and wilt do that which is right in
His eyes, and wilt give ear to His commandments, and
keep all His statutes, I will put none of the diseases
upon thee, which I have put upon the Egyptians: for I
am the Lord that *healeth* thee. (Exodus 15 :22-26.)

SICKNESS REMOVED BY SERVING GOD

Behold, I will send an angel before thee, to keep
thee by the way, and to bring thee into the place which
I have prepared.   Take ye heed before him, and
hearken unto his voice; provoke him not; for he will
not pardon your transgression: for my name is in him.
But if thou shalt indeed hearken unto his voice, and do
all that I speak; then I will be an enemy unto thine
enemies, and an adversary unto thine adversaries.   For
mine angel shall go before thee, and bring thee in unto
the Amorite, and the Hittite, and the Perizzite, and the
Canaanite, the Hivite, and the Jebusite: and I will cut
them off.   Thou shalt not bow down to their gods, nor

serve them, nor do after their works; but thou shalt utterly overthrow them, and break in pieces their pillars. And ye shall serve the Lord, your God, and he will bless thy bread, and thy water; and *I will take sickness away from the midst of thee.* (Exodus 23 :20-25.)

MIRIAM SMITTEN WITH LEPROSY AND HEALED BY PRAYER OF MOSES

And Miriam and Aaron spake against Moses because of the Cushite woman whom he had married; for he had married a Cushite woman. And they said, Hath the Lord indeed spoken only with Moses? Hath he not spoken also with us? And the Lord heard it. Now the man Moses was very meek, above all the men that were upon the face of the earth.

And the Lord spake suddenly unto Moses, and unto Aaron, and unto Miriam, Come out ye three unto the tent of meeting. And they three came out. And the Lord came down in a pillar of cloud, and stood at the door of the Tent, and called Aaron and Miriam; and they both came forth. And he said, Hear now my words: if there be a prophet among you, I, the Lord, will make myself known unto him in a vision, I will speak with him in a dream. My servant Moses is not so; he is faithful in all my house: with him will I speak mouth to mouth, even manifestly, and not in dark speeches; and the form of the Lord shall he behold: wherefore then were ye not afraid to speak against my servant, against Moses.

And the anger of the Lord was kindled against them; and he departed. And the cloud removed from over the Tent; and, behold, Miriam was leprous, as white as snow: and Aaron looked upon Miriam, and, behold, she was leprous. And Aaron said unto Moses, O, my lord, lay not, I pray thee, sin upon us, for that we have done foolishly, and for that we have sinned. Let her not, I pray, be as one dead, And Moses cried unto the Lord saying, *Heal her,* O God, I beseech thee. And the Lord said unto Moses, If her father had but spit in her face, should she not be ashamed seven days? Let her be shut up without the camp seven days, and after that she shall be brought in again. And Miriam was shut up without the camp seven days, and the people journeyed not till Miriam was brought in again. (Numbers, Chapter 12.)

GOD TAKES AWAY ALL SICKNESS FROM ISRAEL WHEN HE KEEPS HIS COVENANT

Know therefore that the Lord thy God, he is God, the faithful God, who keepeth covenant and loving kindness with them that love Him and keep His commandments to a thousand generations, and repayeth them that hate Him to their face, to destroy them: He will not be slack to him that hateth Him, He will repay him to his face. Thou shalt therefore keep the commandment, and the statutes, and the ordinances, which I command thee this day, to do them.

And it shall come to pass, because ye hearken to these ordinances, and keep and do them, that the Lord thy God will keep with thee the covenant and the loving kindness which he sware unto thy fathers: and He will love thee, and bless thee, and multiply thee; He will also bless the fruit of thy body and the fruit of thy ground, thy grain and thy new wine and thine oil, the increase of thy cattle and the young of thy flock, in the land which he sware unto thy fathers to give thee.

Thou shalt be blessed above all peoples: there shall not be male or female barren among you, or among your cattle. *And the Lord will take away from thee all sickness;* and none of the evil diseases of Egypt, which thou knowest, will be put upon thee, but will lay them upon all them that hate thee. (Deuteronomy 7: 9-15.)

GOD, THE ONLY HEALER

See now that I, even I, am He, And there is no god with Me: I kill, and I make alive; I wound, and I *heal.* And there is none that can deliver out of my hand. (Deuteronomy 32 :39.)

HANNAH'S PRAYER FOR A SON

Now there was a certain man of Ramathaimzophim, of Mount Ephraim, and his name was Elkanah, the son of Jeroham, the son of Elihu, the son of Tohu, the son of Zuph, an Ephrathite: And he had two wives; the name of the one was Hannah, and the name of the other Peninnah: and Peninnah had children, but Hannah had no children. And this man went up out of his city yearly to worship and to sacrifice unto the Lord of hosts in Shiloh. And the two sons of Eli, Hophni and Phinehas, the priests of the Lord, were there.

And when the time was that Elkanah offered, he gave to Peninnah his wife, and to all her sons and her daughters, portions: But unto Hannah he gave a worthy portion: for he loved Hannah. And her adversary also provoked her sore, to make her fret. And as he did so year by year, when she went up to the house of the Lord, so she provoked her; therefore she wept, and did not eat. Then said Elkanah her husband to her, Hannah, why weepest thou? and why eatest thou not? and why is thy heart grieved? Am not I better to thee than ten sons?

So Hannah rose up after they had eaten in Shiloh, and after they had drunk. Now Eli the priest sat upon a seat by a post of the temple of the Lord. And she was in bitterness of soul, and prayed unto the Lord, and wept sore. And she vowed a vow, and said, O Lord of hosts, if thou wilt indeed look on the affliction of thine handmaid, and remember me, and not forget thine handmaid, but wilt give unto thine handmaid a man child, then I will give him unto the Lord all the days of his life, and there shall no razor come upon his head.

And it came to pass, as she continued praying before the Lord, that Eli marked her mouth. Now Hannah, spake in her heart: only her lips moved, but her voice was not heard: therefore Eli thought she had been drunken. And Eli said unto her, How long wilt thou be drunken? Put away thy wine from thee. And Hannah, answered and said, No, my lord, I am a woman of a sorrowful spirit: I have drunk neither wine nor strong drink, but have poured out my soul before the Lord. Count not thine handmaid for a daughter of Belial; for out of the abundance of my complaint and grief have I spoken hitherto. Then Eli answered and said, Go in peace: and the God of Israel grant thee thy petition that thou hast asked of him. And she said, Let thine handmaid find grace in thy sight. So the woman went her way, and did eat, and her countenance was no more sad.

And they rose up in the morning early, and worshipped before the Lord, and returned, and came to their house to Ramah: and Elkanah knew Hannah his wife: and the Lord remembered her. Wherefore it came to pass, when the time was come about after Hannah had conceived, that she bare a son, and called his name Samuel, saying, Because I have asked him of the Lord. And the man Elkanah, and all his house, went up to offer unto the Lord the yearly sacrifice, and his vow. But Hannah went not up; for she said unto her husband, I will not go up until the child be weaned, and then I will bring him, that he may appear before the Lord, and there abide forever.

And Elkanah her husband said unto her, Do what seemeth thee good; tarry until thou have weaned him; only the Lord establish his word. And when she had weaned him, she took him up with her, with three bullocks, and one ephah of flour, and a bottle of wine, and brought him unto the house of the Lord in Shiloh: and the child was young. And they slew a bullock, and brought the child to Eli. And she said, O my Lord, as thy soul liveth, my Lord, I am the woman that stood by thee here, praying unto the Lord. For this child I prayed: and the Lord hath given me my petition which I asked of him: Therefore also I have lent him to the Lord: as long as he liveth he shall be lent to the Lord. And she worshipped the Lord there. (1 Samuel, Chapter 1.)

THE PHILISTINES HEALED BY GOD, AFTER THEY HAD SENT BACK THE ARK OF THE COVENANT

Now, the Philistines had taken the ark of God, and they brought it from Ebenezer unto Ashdod. And the Philistines took the ark of God, and brought it into the house of Dagon, and set it by Dagon. And when they of Ashdod arose early on the morrow, behold, Dagon was fallen upon his face to the ground before the ark of the

Lord. And they took Dagon, and set him in his place
again. And when they arose early on the morrow
morning, behold, Dagon was fallen upon his face to the
ground before the ark of the Lord; and the head of
Dagon and both the palms of his hands lay cut off
upon the threshold; only the stump of Dagon was left
to him. Therefore neither the priests of Dagon, nor any
that come into Dagon's house, tread on the threshold of
Dagon in Ashdod, unto this day.

But the hand of the Lord was heavy upon them of
Ashdod, and he destroyed them, and smote them with
tumors, even Ashdod and the borders thereof. And
when the men of Ashdod saw that it was so, they said,
The ark of the God of Israel shall not abide with us; for
His hand is sore upon us, and upon Dagon our god.
They sent therefore and gathered all the lords of the
Philistines unto them, and said, What shall we do with
the ark of the God of Israel? And they answered, Let
the ark of the God of Israel be carried about unto Gath.
And they carried the ark of the God of Israel thither.
And it was so, that, after they had carried it about, the
hand of the Lord was against the city with a very great
discomfiture: and He smote the men of the city, both
small and great; and tumors brake out upon them. So
they sent the ark of God to Ekron. And it came to
pass, as the ark of God came to Ekron, that the
Ekronites cried out, saying, They have brought about
the ark of the God of Israel to us, to slay us and our
people. They sent therefore and gathered together all
the lords of the Philistines, and they said, Send away
the ark of the God of Israel, and let it go again to its
own place, that it slay us not, and our people. For
there was a deadly discomfiture throughout all the
city; the hand of God was very heavy there. And the
men that died not were smitten with the tumors; and

the cry of the city went up to heaven. And the ark of the Lord was in the country of the Philistines seven months. And the Philistines called for the priests and the diviners, saying, What shall we do with the ark of the Lord? Show us wherewith we shall send it to its place. And they said, If ye send away the ark of the God of Israel, send it not empty; but by all means return Him a trespass offering: then ye shall be *healed,* and it shall be known to you why his hand is not removed from you. (1 Samuel, Chapters 5 and 6, re-arranged.)

ELIJAH BY FAITH HEALS THE WIDOW'S SON

And the word of the Lord came unto him, saying, Arise, get thee to Zarephath, which belongeth to Sidon, and dwell there: behold, I have commanded a widow there to sustain thee. So he arose and went to Zarephath: and when he came to the gate of the city, behold, a widow was there gathering sticks; and he called to her, and said, Fetch me, I pray thee, a little water in a vessel, that I may drink. And as she was going to fetch it, he called to her, and said, Bring me, I pray thee, a morsel of bread in thy hand, And she said, As the Lord, thy God liveth, I have not a cake, but a handful of meal in the jar, and a little oil in the cruse: and, behold, I am gathering two sticks, that I may go in and dress it for me and my son, that we may eat it, and die. And Elijah said unto her, Fear not; go and do as thou hast said; but make me thereof a little cake first, and bring it forth unto me, and afterward make for thee and for thy son. For thus saith the Lord, the God of Israel. The jar of meal shall not waste, neither shall the cruse of oil fail, until the day that the Lord sendeth rain upon the earth. And she went and did according to the saying of Elijah: and she, and he, and her house, did eat many days. The jar of meal wasted not, neither did the cruse of oil fail, according to the word of the Lord, which he spake by Elijah. And it came to pass after these things, that the son of the woman, the mistress of the house, fell sick; and his sickness was so sore, that there was no breath left in him. And she said unto Elijah, What have I to do with thee, O thou man of God? Thou art come unto me to bring my sin to remembrance and to slay my son! And he said unto her, Give me thy son. And he took him out of her bosom, and carried him up into the chamber, where he abode, and laid him upon his own bed. And he cried unto the Lord, and said, O Lord, my God, hast thou also brought evil upon the widow with whom I sojourn, by slaying her son? And he stretched himself upon the child three times, and cried unto the Lord and said, O, Lord, my God, I pray thee, let this child's soul come into him again. And the Lord hearkened unto the voice of Elijah; and the soul of the child came into him again, and he revived. And Elijah took the child, and brought him down out of the chamber into the house, and delivered him unto his mother; and Elijah said, *See, thy son, liveth.* And the woman said to Elijah, Now I know that thou art a man of God, and that the word of the Lord in thy mouth is truth. (1 Kings, Chapter 17 :8-24.)

AHAZIAH, KING OF ISRAEL, DIES BECAUSE OF HIS PRAYER TO A FALSE GOD BAALZEBUB

And Moab rebelled against Israel after the death of Ahab, and Ahaziah fell down through the lattice in his upper chamber that was in Samaria, and was sick; and he sent messengers, and said unto them, Go, inquire of

Baal-Zebub, the god of Ekron, whether I shall recover of this sickness. But the Lord said to Elijah the Tishbite, Arise, go up to meet the messengers of the king of Samaria, and say unto them, Is it because there is no God in Israel, that ye go to inquire of Baal-Zebub, the god of Ekron? Now therefore thus saith the Lord, Thou shalt not come down from the bed whither thou art gone up, but shalt surely die. And Elijah departed.

And the messengers, returned unto him, and he said unto them, Why is it that ye are returned? And they said unto him, There came up a man to meet us, and said unto us, Go, turn again unto the king that sent you, and say unto him, Thus saith the Lord, Is it because there is no God in Israel that thou sendest to inquire of Baal-Zebub, the god of Ekron? therefore thou shalt not come down from the bed whither thou art gone up, but shalt surely die. And he said unto them, What manner of man was he that came up to meet you, and told you these words? And they answered him. He was a hairy man, and girt with a girdle of leather about his loins. And he said, It is Elijah the Tishbite.

Then the king sent unto him a captain of fifty with his fifty. And he went up to him: and, behold, he was sitting on the top of the hill. And he spake unto him, O man of God, the king hath said, Come down. And Elijah answered and said to the captain of fifty, If I be a man of God, let fire come down from heaven, and consume thee and thy fifty. And there came down fire from heaven, and consumed him and his fifty. And again he sent unto him another captain of fifty with his fifty. And he answered and said unto him, O man of God, thus hath the king said, Come down quickly. And Elijah answered and said unto them, If I be a man of God, let fire come down from heaven and consume thee and thy fifty. And the fire of God came down from heaven, and consumed him and his fifty. And again he sent the captain of a third fifty with his fifty. And the third captain of fifty went up, and came and fell on his knees before Elijah, and besought him, and said unto him, O man of God, I pray thee, let my life, and the life of these fifty thy servants, be precious in thy sight. Behold, there came fire down from heaven, and consumed the two former captains of fifty with their fifties; but now let my life be precious in thy sight. And the angel of God said unto Elijah, Go down with him: be not afraid of him. And he arose, and went down with him unto the king. And he said unto him, Thus saith the Lord, Forasmuch as thou hast sent messengers to inquire of Baal-Zebub, the god of Ekron, *is it because there is no God in Israel to inquire of his word?* Therefore thou shalt not come down from the bed whither thou art gone up, but shalt surely die. And when he had called her, she stood before him. And he said unto him, Say now unto her, Behold, thou hast been careful for us with all this care; what is to be done for thee? Wouldest thou be spoken for to the king, or to the captain of the host? And she answered, I dwell among mine own people. And he said, What then is to be done for her? And Gehazi answered, Verily she hath no son, and her husband is old. And he said, Call her. And when he had called her, she stood in the door. And he said, At this season, when the time cometh round, thou shalt embrace a son. And she said, Nay, my lord, thou man of God, do not lie unto thy handmaid.

So he died according to the word of the Lord, which Elijah had spoken. (2 Kings, Chapter 1 : 1-17.)

ELISHA HEALS THE SON OF THE SHUNAMMITE WOMAN

And it fell on a day, that Elisha passed to Shuhem, where was a great woman; and she constrained him to eat bread. And so it was, that as oft as he passed by, he turned in thither to eat bread. And she said unto her husband, Behold now, I perceive that this is a holy man of God, that passeth by us continually. Let us make, I pray thee, a little chamber on the wall; let us set for him there a bed, and a table, and a seat, and a candlestick; and it shall be, when he cometh to us, that he shall turn in thither. And it fell on a day, that he came thither, and he turned into the chamber and lay there. And he said to Gehazi his servant, Call this Shunammite.

And the woman conceived, and bare a son at that season, when the time came round, as Elisha had said unto her. And when the child was grown, it fell on a day, that he went out to his father to the reapers. And he said unto his father, My head, my head. And he said to his servant, Carry him to his mother. And when he had taken him, and brought him to his mother, he sat on her knees till noon, and then died. And she went up and laid him on the bed of the man of God, and shut the door upon him, and went out. And she called unto her husband and said, Send me, I pray thee, one of the servants, and one of the asses, that I may run to the man of God, and come again. And he said, Wherefore wilt thou go to him today? It is neither new moon nor Sabbath. And she said, It shall be well. Then she saddled an ass, and said to her servant, Drive, and go forward; slacken me not the riding, except I bid thee. So she went, and came unto the man of God to mount Carmel.

And it came to pass, when the man of God saw her afar off, that he said to Gehazi his servant, Behold, yonder is the Shunammite: run, I pray thee, now to meet her, and say unto her, Is it well with thee? Is it well with thy husband? Is it well with the child? And she answered, It is well. And when she came to the man of God to the hill, she caught hold of his feet. And Gehazi came near to thrust her away; but the man of God said, Let her alone: for her soul is vexed within her; and the Lord hath hid it from me and hath not told me. Then she said, Did I desire a son of my lord? Did I not say, Do not deceive me? Then he said to Gehazi, Gird up thy loins, and take my staff in thy hand, and go thy way: if thou meet any man, salute him not; and if any salute thee, answer him not again: and lay my staff upon the face of the child. And the mother of the child said, As the Lord liveth, and as thy soul liveth, I will not leave thee. And he arose, and followed her. And Gehazi passed on before them, and laid the staff upon the face of the child; but there was neither voice nor hearing. Wherefore he returned to meet him, and told him, saying, The child is not awaked.

And when Elisha was come into the house, behold, the child was dead, and laid upon his bed. He went in therefore, and shut the door upon them twain, and *prayed unto the Lord.* And he went up, and lay upon the child, and put his mouth upon his mouth, and his eyes upon his eyes, and his hands upon his hands: and he stretched himself upon him: and the flesh of the child waxed warm. Then he returned, and walked in the house once to and fro; and went up, and stretched himself, upon him: and the child sneezed seven times, and *the child opened his eyes.* And he called Gehazi, and said, Call this Shunammite. So he called her. And when she was come in unto him, he said, Take up thy son. Then she went in, and fell at his feet, and bowed herself to the ground; and she took up her son, and went out. (2 Kings 4 :8-37.)

NAAMAN AND THE HOUSE OF RIMMON

Now Naaman, captain of the host of the king of Syria, was a great man with his master, and honorable, because by him the Lord had given deliverance unto Syria; he was also a mighty man in valor, but he was a leper. And the Syrians had gone out in bands, and had brought away captive out of the land of Israel a little maiden; and she waited on Naaman's wife. And she said unto her mistress, Would that my lord were with the prophet that is in Samaria! Then would he recover him of his leprosy. And one went in, and told his lord, saying, Thus and thus said the maiden that is of the land of Israel. And the king of Syria said, Go now, and I will send a letter unto the king of Israel. And he departed, and took with him ten talents of silver, and six thousand pieces of gold, and ten changes of raiment. And he brought the letter to the king of Israel, saying, And now when this letter is come unto thee, behold, I have sent Naaman my servant to thee, that thou mayest recover him of his leprosy. And it came to pass, when the king of Israel had read the letter, that he rent his clothes, and said, Am I god, to kill and to make alive, that this man doth send unto me to recover a man of his leprosy? But consider, I pray you, and see how he seeketh a quarrel against me.

And it was so, when Elisha the man of God heard that the king of Israel had rent his clothes, that he sent to the king, saying, Wherefore hast thou rent thy clothes? Let him come now to me, and he shall know that there is a prophet in Israel. So Naaman came with his horses and with his chariots, and stood at the door of the house of Elisha. And Elisha sent a messenger unto him, saying, Go and wash in the Jordon seven times, and thy flesh shall come again to thee, and thou shalt be clean. But Naaman was wroth, and went away, and said, Behold, I thought, He will surely come out to me, and stand, and call on the name of the Lord his God, and strike his hand over the place, and recover the leper.

Are not Abana and Pharpar, rivers of Damascus, better than all the waters of Israel? May I not wash in them, and be clean? So he turned and went away in a rage. And his servants came near, and spake unto him, and said, My father, if the prophet had bid thee do some great thing, wouldest thou not have done it? how much rather then, when he saith to thee, Wash, and be clean? Then went he down, and dipped himself seven times in Jordon, according to the saying of the man of God; *and his flesh came again like unto the flesh of a little child, and he was clean.* And he returned to the man of God, he and all his company, and came, and stood before him: and he said, Behold, now I know that there is no God in all the earth, but in Israel: now therefore, I pray thee, take a blessing of thy servant. But he said, as the Lord liveth, before whom I stand, I will receive none. And he urged him to take it; but he refused. And Naaman said, If not, yet, I pray thee, let there be given to thy servant two mules' burden of earth; for thy servant will henceforth offer neither burnt-offering nor sacrifice unto other gods, but unto the Lord. In this thing the Lord pardon thy servant: when my master goeth into the house of Rimmon to worship there, and he leaneth on my hand, and I bow myself in the house of Rimmon, when I bow myself in the house of Rimmon, the Lord pardon thy servant in this thing. And he said unto him, Go in peace. So he departed from him a little way.

But Gehazi, the servant of Elisha the man of God, said Behold, my master hath spared this Naaman the Syrian, in not receiving at his hands that which he brought: as the Lord liveth, I will run after him, and take somewhat of him. So Gehazi followed after Naaman. And when Naaman saw one running after him, he alighted from the chariot to meet him, and said, Is all well? And he said, All is well. My master hath sent me, saying, Behold, even now there are come to me from the hill-country of Ephrain two young men of the sons of the prophets; give them, I pray thee, a talent of silver, and two changes of raiment. And Naaman said, Be pleased to take two talents. And he urged him, and bound two talents of silver in two bags, with two changes of raiment, and laid them upon two of his servants; and they bare them before him. And when he came to the hill, he took them from their hand, and bestowed them in the house; and he let the men go, and they departed. But he went in, and stood before his master. And Elisha said unto him, Whence comest thou, Gehazi? And he said, Thy servant went no whither. And he said unto him, Went not my heart with thee, when the man turned from his chariot to meet thee? Is it a time to receive money, and to receive garments, and olive yards and vineyards, and sheep and oxen, and men-servants and maid-servants? The leprosy therefore of Naaman shall cleave unto thee, and unto thy seed forever. And he went out from his presence a leper as white as snow. (2 Kings, Chapter 5.)

BENHADAD, KING OF SYRIA, SEEKS THE HEALING INFLUENCE OF ELISHA, THE MAN OF GOD

And Elisha came to Damascus; and Benhadad the king of Syria was sick; and it was told him, saying, The man of God is come hither. And the king said unto Hazael, Take a present in thy hand, and go, meet the man of God, and inquire of the Lord by him, saying, Shall I recover of this sickness? So Hazael went to meet him, and took a present with him, even of every good thing of Damascus, forty camels' burden, and came and stood before him, and said, Thy son Benhadad king of Syria hath sent me to thee, saying, Shall I recover of this sickness? And Elisha said unto him, Go, say unto him, Thou shalt surely recover; howbeit the Lord hath showed me that he shall surely die. And he settled his countenance steadfastly upon him, until he was ashamed; and the man of God wept. And Hazael said, Why weepeth my lord? And he answered, Because I know the evil that thou wilt do unto the children of Israel: their strongholds wilt thou set on fire, and their young men wilt thou slay with the sword, and wilt dash in pieces their little ones, and rip up their women with child. And Hazael said, But what is thy servant, who is but a dog, that he should do this great thing? And Elisha answered, the Lord hath showed me that thou shalt be king over Syria. Then he departed from Elisha, and came to his master; who said to him, What said Elisha to thee? And he answered, He told me that thou wouldest surely recover. And it came to pass on the morrow, that he took the coverlet and dipped it in water, and spread it on his face, so that he died: and Hazael reigned in his stead. (2 Kings 8 :7-15.)

HEZEKIAH'S PRAYER FOR HEALING

In those days was Hezekiah sick unto death. And Isaiah the prophet the son of Amos came to him, and said unto him, Thus saith the Lord, Set thy house in order; for thou shalt die, and not live. Then he turned his face to the wall, and prayed unto the Lord saying, Remember now, O Lord, I beseech thee, how I have walked before thee in truth and with a perfect heart, and have done that which is good in thy sight. And Hezekiah wept sore. And it came to pass, before Isaiah was gone out into the middle part of the city, that the word of the Lord came to him, saying, Turn back, and say to Hezekiah the prince of my people, Thus saith the Lord, the God of David thy father, *I have heard thy prayer, I have seen thy tears; behold, I will Heal thee;* on the third day thou shalt go up into the house of the Lord. And I will add unto thy days fifteen years; and I will deliver thee and this city out of the hand of the king of Assyria; and I will defend this city for mine own sake, and for my servant David's sake. And Isaiah said, Take a cake of figs. And they took and laid it on the boil, and he recovered. (2 Kings 20 : 1-7.)

EGYPT HEALED BY GOD

In that day shall there be an altar to the Lord in the midst of the land of Egypt, and a pillar at the border thereof to the Lord. And it shall be for a sign and for a witness unto the Lord in the land of Egypt; for they shall cry unto the Lord because of oppressors, and he will send them a savior, and a defender, and He will deliver them. And the Lord shall be known to Egypt, and the Egyptians shall know the Lord in that day;

yea, they shall worship with sacrifice and oblation, and shall vow a vow unto the Lord and shall perform it. And the Lord will smite Egypt, smiting and *healing;* and they shall return unto the Lord, and he will be entreated of them, and will *heal* them. (Isaiah Chap. 19:19-22.)

HEALING ONLY THROUGH THE LORD

A glorious throne, set on high from the beginning, is the place of our sanctuary. O Lord, the hope of Israel, all that forsake thee shall be put to shame. They that depart from me shall be written in the earth, because they have forsaken the Lord, the foundation of living waters. *Heal me, O Lord, and I shall be healed; save me, and I shall be saved: for Thou art my praise.* Behold they say unto me, where is the word of the Lord? Let it come now. As for me, I have not hastened from being a shepherd after thee; neither have I desired the woeful day; Thou knowest: that which came out of my lips was before Thy face. Be not a terror unto me: thou art my refuge in the day of evil. (Jeremiah, Chapter 17:12-17.)

EZEKIEL REBUKES THE SHEPHERDS OF ISRAEL FOR NOT HEALING THE SICK

And the word of the Lord came unto me, saying, son of man, prophesy against the shepherds of Israel, prophesy, and say unto them, even to the shepherds, Thus saith the Lord God: Woe unto the shepherds of Israel that do feed themselves! Should not the shepherds feed the sheep? Ye eat the fat, and ye clothe you with the wool, ye kill the fatlings; but ye feed not the sheep. The diseased have ye not strengthened, neither have ye *healed* that which was sick, neither have ye bound up that which was broken, neither have ye brought back that which was driven away, neither have ye sought that which was lost; but with force and with rigor have ye ruled over them. And they were scattered, because there was no shepherd; and they became food to all the beasts of the field, and were scattered. My sheep wandered through all the mountains, and upon every high hill: yea, my sheep were scattered upon all the face of the earth; and there was none that did search or seek after them. (Ezekiel, Chapter 34 : 1-6.)

THE WONDERFUL VISION OF THE DRY BONES

The hand of the Lord was upon me, and he brought me out in the spirit, and set me down in the midst of the valley; and it was full of bones. And he caused me to pass by them round about; and, behold, there were very many in the open valley; and lo, they were very dry. And he said unto me, Son of man, can these bones live? And I answered, O Lord God, thou knowest. Again he said unto me, Prophesy over these bones, and say unto them, O ye dry bones, hear the word of the Lord. Thus saith the Lord God unto these bones: Behold, I will cause breath to enter into you, and ye shall live. And I will lay sinews upon you, and will bring up flesh upon you, and cover you with skin, and put breath in you, and *ye shall live: and ye shall know that I am the Lord.*

So I prophesied as I was commanded: and as I prophesied, there was a noise, and, behold, an earthquake; and the bones came together, bone to its bone. And I beheld, and lo, there were sinews upon them, and flesh came up, and skin covered them above; but there was no breath in them. Then said he unto me, Prophesy unto the wind, prophesy, son of man, and say to the wind, Thus saith the Lord God: Come from the four winds, O breath, and breathe upon these slain, that they may live. So I prophesied as he commanded me, and the breath came into them, and they lived, and stood up upon their feet, an exceeding great army.

Then he said unto me, Son of man, these bones are the whole house of Israel: behold, they say, Our bones are dried up, and our hope is lost; we are clean cut off. Therefore prophesy, and say unto them, Thus saith the Lord God; Behold, I will open your graves, and cause you to come up out of your graves, O my people; and I will bring you into the land of Israel. And ye shall know that I am the Lord, when I have opened your graves, and caused you to come up out of your graves, O my people. And I will put my spirit in you, and ye shall live, and I will place you in your own land; and ye shall know that I, the Lord, have spoken it and performed it. (Ezekiel 37: 1-14.)

GOD HEALS THE SMITTEN

Come and let us return unto the Lord; for he hath torn, and he will *heal* us; he hath smitten, and he will bind us up. After two days will He revive us: on the third day He will raise us up, *and we shall live before Him.* And let us know, let us follow on to know the Lord; His going forth is sure as the morning; and he will come unto us as the rain, as the latter rain that watereth the earth. (Hosea 6 : 1-3.)

THE SUN OF RIGHTEOUSNESS WITH HEALING
ON ITS WINGS

For, behold, the day cometh, it burneth as a furnace; and all the proud, and all that work wickedness, shall be stubble; and the day that cometh shall burn them up, saith the Lord of hosts, that it shall leave them neither root nor branch. But unto you that fear My name shall the sun of righteousness arise with *healing* in its wings; and ye shall go forth, and gambol as calves of the stall. And ye shall tread down the wicked; for they shall be ashes under the soles of your feet in the day that I make, saith the Lord God of hosts. (Malachi 4:1-3.)

A PRAYER FOR DIVINE HEALING

O Lord, rebuke me not in thine anger,
    Neither chasten me in thy hot displeasure.
Have mercy upon me, O Lord; for I am withered away:
    O Lord, *heal* me; for my bones are troubled.
My soul also is sore troubled:
    And thou, O Lord, how long?
Return, O Lord, deliver my soul:
    Save me for thy loving kindness' sake.
For in death there is no remembrance of thee:
    In Sheol who shall give thee thanks?
I am weary with my groaning;
    Every night make I my bed to swim;
I water my couch with my tears.
    Mine eye wasteth away because of grief;
It waxeth old because of all mine adversaries.
    Depart from me, all ye workers of iniquity;
For the Lord hath heard the voice of my weeping.

The Lord hath heard my supplication;
The Lord will receive my prayer.

    All mine enemies shall be put to shame and sore
        troubled:
They shall turn back, they shall be put to shame
suddenly.   (The Sixth Psalm.)

THE PSALM OF FAITH

The Lord is my shepherd: I shall not want.
    He maketh me to lie down in green pastures;
He leadeth me beside still waters.
    He restoreth my soul:
He guideth me in the paths of righteousness for his
        name's sake.
    Yea, though I walk through the valley of the
        shadow of death,
I will fear no evil; for thou art with me;
    Thy rod and thy staff, they comfort me.
Thou preparest a table before me in the presence of
        mine enemies;
    Thou hast anointed my head with oil;
My cup runneth over.
    Surely goodness and loving kindness shall follow
        me all the days of my life;
And I shall dwell in the house of the Lord forever.
                 The Twenty-Third Psalm.)

A PRAYER OF THANKSGIVING FOR
DELIVERANCE FROM DEATH

I will extol thee, O Lord, for thou hast raised me up,
    And hast not made my foes to rejoice over me.
O Lord, my God, I cried unto thee, and thou hast
    healed me.

O God, thou hast brought up my soul from Sheol;
Thou hast kept me alive, that I should not go down to
      the pit.
     Sing praise unto the Lord, O ye saints of His,
And give thanks to His holy memorial name.
     For His anger is but for a moment;
His favor is for a life-time:
     Weeping may tarry for the night,
But joy cometh in the morning.
     As for me, I said in my prosperity,
I shall never be moved.
     Thou O Lord, of Thy favor hadst made my
      mountain to stand strong;
Thou didst hide Thy face; I was troubled.
     I cried to thee, O Lord;
And unto the Lord I made supplication:
     What profit is there in my blood, when I go down to
      the pit?
Shall the dust praise thee? Shall it declare thy truth?
     Hear O Lord, and have mercy upon me;
Lord, be thou my helper.
     Thou hast turned for me my mourning into dancing;
Thou hast loosed my sackcloth, and girded me with
      gladness;
     To the end that my glory may sing praise to thee,
      and not be silent.
O Lord, my God, I will give thanks unto thee for ever.
               (The Thirtieth Psalm.)

DIVINE HEALING FOR HIM WHO BEFRIENDS
THE POOR

Blessed is he that considereth the poor:
     The Lord will deliver him in the day of evil.
The Lord will preserve him, and keep him alive.

And he shall be blessed upon the earth;
And deliver not thou him into the will of his enemies.
    The Lord will support him upon the couch of
        languishing:
Thou makest all his bed in his sickness.

(Psalm 41: 1-3.)

THE PRAYER OF THE PENITENT SICK

O Lord, rebuke me not in Thy wrath;
    Neither chasten me in Thy hot displeasure.
For Thine arrows stick fast in me,
    And Thy hand presseth me sore.
There is no soundness in my flesh because of Thine
        indignation;
    Neither is there any health in my bones because of
        my sin.
For mine iniquities are gone over my head;
    As a heavy burden they are too heavy for me.
My wounds are loathsome and corrupt,
    Because of my foolishness.
I am pained and bowed down greatly;
    I go mourning all the day long.
For my loins are filled with burning;
    And there is no soundness in my flesh.
I am faint and sore bruised:
    I have groaned by reason of the disquietness of my
        heart.
Lord all my desire is before thee;
    And my groaning is not hid from thee.
My heart throbbeth, my strength faileth me:
    As for the light of mine eyes, it also is gone from
        me.
My lovers and my friends stand aloof from my plague;
    And my kinsmen stand afar off.

They also that seek after my life lay snares for me;
    And they that seek my hurt speak mischievous
        things,
And meditate deceits all the day long.
    But I, as a deaf man, hear not;
And I am as a dumb man that openeth not his mouth,
    Yea, I am as a man that heareth not,
And in whose mouth are no reproofs.
    For in Thee, O Lord, do I hope;
Thou wilt answer, O Lord, my God.
    For I said, Lest they rejoice over me:
When my foot slippeth, they magnify themselves
        against me.
    For I am ready to fall,
And my sorrow is continually before *me.*
    For I will declare mine iniquity;
I will be sorry for my sin.
    But mine enemies are lively, and are strong;
And they that hate me wrongfully are multiplied.
    They also that render evil for good
Are adversaries unto me, because I follow the thing
        that is good.
    Forsake me not, O Lord;
O my God, be not far from me.
    Make haste to help me,
O Lord, my salvation.

                    (The Thirty-Eighth Psalm.)

PRAISE OF GOD, WHO HEALS DISEASES

Bless the Lord, O my soul;
    And all that is within me, bless His holy name.
Bless the Lord, O my soul,
    And forget not all His benefits:
Who forgiveth all thine iniquities:

Who *healeth* all thy diseases;
Who redeemeth thy life from destruction;
    Who crowneth thee with loving kindness and
        tender mercies;
Who satisfieth thy desire with good things,
    So that thy youth is renewed like the eagle.

                        (Psalm 103:1-5.)

THE LORD SAVETH HIS PEOPLE FROM SICKNESS AND DEATH

Oh give thanks unto the Lord; for He is good;
    For His loving kindness endureth for ever.
Let the redeemed of the Lord say,
    Whom He hath redeemed from the hand of the
        adversary,
And gathered out of the lands,
    From the east and from the west,
From the north and from the south.

They wandered in the wilderness in a desert way;
    They found no city of habitation.
Hungry and thirsty,
    Their soul fainted in them.
Then they cried unto the Lord in their trouble,
    And He delivered them out of their distresses,
He led them also by a straight way,
    That they might go to a city of habitation.
Oh that men would praise the Lord for His kindness,
    And for his wonderful works to the children of men!
For He satisfieth the longing soul,
    And the hungry He filleth with good.
Such as sat in darkness and in the shadow of death,
    Being bound in affiction and iron,
Because they rebelled against the words of God,

And contemned the counsel of the Most High;
Therefore He brought down their heart with labor:
    They fell down, and there was none to help.
Then they cried unto the Lord in their trouble,
    And He saved them out of their distresses.
He brought them out of darkness and the shadow of
        death,
    And brake their bonds in sunder,
Oh that men would praise the Lord for His kindness,
    And for His wonderful works to the children of
        men!
For He hath broken the gates of brass
    And cut the bars of iron asunder.
Then they cried unto the Lord in their trouble,
    And He saved them out of their distresses.
He sendeth His word, and *healeth* them,
    And delivereth them from their destruction.
Oh that men would praise the Lord for His kindness,
    And for His wonderful works to the children of
        men!
And let them offer the sacrifices of thanksgiving,
    And declare His works with singing.

                              (Psalm 107: 1-16, 19-22.)

HEALTH COMES FROM THE FEAR OF GOD

My son, forget not my law;
    But let thy heart keep my commandments;
For length of days, and years of life,
    And peace, will they add to thee.
Let not kindness and truth forsake thee;
    Bind them about thy neck;
Write them upon the tablet of thy heart:
    So shalt thou find favor and good understanding
In the sight of God and man,

Trust in the Lord with all thy heart,
And lean not upon thine own understanding;
In all thy ways acknowledge him,
And He will direct thy paths.
Be not wise in thine own eyes;
Fear the Lord, and depart from evil:
It will be *health* to thy navel,
And marrow to thy bones.

(Proverbs 3: 1-8.)

THE WORDS OF GOD BRING LIFE AND HEALTH

My son, attend to my words;
Incline thine ear unto my sayings.
Let them not depart from thine eyes;
Keep them in the midst of thy heart.
For they are life unto those that find them,
And *health* to all their flesh.

(Proverbs 4: 20-22.)

PRAYERS FOR DIVINE HEALING AND PROTECTION, FROM THE TEFILLAH OR PRAYER BOOK OF ISRAEL

Prayer said on Rising in the Morning:

I give thanks unto Thee, O King, living and established, that Thou hast watched over my soul in sleep. Great is Thy faithfulness.

The prayer known as "Adon Olom" or "The Eternal God:"

The Lord of all did reign supreme
Ere yet this world was made and formed

When all was finished by His will
Then was His name, as King proclaimed.

And should these forms no more exist
He still will rule in majesty
He was, He is, He shall remain.
His glory never shall decrease.

And One is He, and none there is,
To be compared or joined to Him
He ne'er began and ne'er will end
To Him belong Dominion's power.

He is my God, my living God,
To Him I flee when tried in grief
My banner high, my refuge strong
Who hears and answers when I call.

My spirit I commit to Him
My body too, and all I prize
Both, when I sleep and when I wake,
He is with me, I shall not fear.

The Prayer known as "Yigdal Elohim," or "Extolled
    Be the Living God":

Extolled be the living God and praised.
He existeth, but His existence is not bounded by time.
He is One, but there is no unity, like unto His unity.
He is incomprehensible, and his unity is unending.
He hath no material form.
He is incorporeal, and naught that is can be compared
        to Him in holiness.
He existed before all things that are created. He is the
        first but there is no beginning to His existence.

Behold, He is the Lord of the world, and all creation
     revealeth His power and dominion.
The inspiration of prophecy did He bestow on the men
     of His Chosen People.
There never arose a prophet in Israel like unto Moses
     who beheld God's similitude.
A true law hath God given to His people, by the hand
     of His prophet who was faithful in His house.
He will not alter nor change His law for any other.
He beholdeth and knoweth all secret things, and
     vieweth the end of a thing at its beginning.
He resurrecteth the dead in His great mercy.
Blessed be the name of His glory forevermore.

A Prayer called "Elohay Neshomoh" or "My God the
    Soul," setting forth the Divine Source and Control
    of the Pure Spirit of Man:

My God the soul which Thou hast given unto me
came pure from Thee. Thou hast created it; Thou hast
formed it; Thou hast breathed it into me. Thou hast
preserved it in my body and, at the appointed time,
Thou wilt take it from this earth, that it may enter on
the life everlasting. While the soul animates my
being, I will worship Thee, Sovereign of the world, and
Lord of all souls. Blessed art Thou, Oh Lord, who
causeth the spirit to return to the dead.

One of the "Shemoneh Esreh" or "Seventeen
    Benedictions." A characteristic Jewish Prayer for
    Divine Help and Healing:

Thou are mighty, Oh Lord, who resurrecteth the
dead, Thou art strong in salvation. In Thy kindness,
Thou sustainest the living, upholdest the fallen,

healest the sick and settest captives free. Thou wilt, of a surety, fulfill Thy promise of immortal life unto those who sleep in the dust. Who is like unto Thee, Almighty, who slayeth and revivest, Thou, who sendeth salvation. Who is like unto Thee, Father of mercy, who remembereth Thy children unto life eternal. Praise be Thou, who resurrecteth the dead.

A Daily Prayer Bespeaking Faith in God as the Source of Life:

We gratefully acknowledge, O Lord, our God, that Thou art our Creator and Preserver, the rock of our life, and the shield of our help. We render thanks unto Thee for our lives, which are in Thy hands, for our souls which are ever in Thy keeping, for Thy wonders which Thou dost perform each day among us, and for Thy continuous goodness which Thou bestowest upon us, day by day. Truly, Thy mercies never fail, and Thy loving kindness never ceases. Therefore in Thee do we forever put our trust.

The Daily Prayer for Peace, Blessing and Life:

Grant us peace, blessing, favor, mercy and loving kindness to us and all Israel, Thy people. Bless all of us, O Father, in the light of Thy countenance, for in Thy light Thou hast given us the Law of life and love, righteousness and blessing, mercy and peace. It is fitting that Thou shouldest bless Thy people Israel at all times and places with Thy peace. Blessed art Thou, O Lord, who blesseth Thy people Israel with peace.

A Typical "Berochoh" or "Blessing," Describing God as
the Divine Healer:

Blessed art Thou, O Lord, who *healeth* all flesh,
and worketh wonders.

Other "Berochoth" or "Blessings":

Blessed art Thou, O Lord, our God, King of the
Universe, who openeth the eyes of the blind.

Blessed art Thou, O Lord, our God, King of the
Universe, who setteth the captives free.

Blessed art Thou, O Lord, our God, King of the
Universe, who upholdeth the falling.

Blessed art Thou, O Lord, our God, King of the
Universe, who guideth the steps of man.

Blessed art Thou, O Lord, our God, King of the
Universe, who giveth strength to the weary.

A Beautiful Evening Prayer, said on Retiring:

Let us lie down in peace, O Lord, our God. Let us
rise, our King, unto life. Spread over us the tabernacle
of Thy peace, and build us up with Thy good counsel.
Save us for Thy own sake. Be Thou a shield about us,
and remove from us the enemy and pestilence, the
sword, famine and grief. Remove the adversary from
before and behind us. Let us hide in the shadow of
Thy wing. Thou art our God, who guardeth and
delivereth us, for Thou art a gracious and merciful
King. Guard our going out and our coming in with life
and peace evermore. Blessed art Thou O Lord, who
guardeth Thy people, Israel, forever.

Another Prayer to be said at the bedside:

Blessed art Thou, O Lord, who causeth the shades of sleep to fall upon my eyes, and slumber on my eyelids. Mayest Thou let us lie down in peace, and arise in peace. Let no evil fancies, thoughts or dreams disturb me, and may my couch be perfect in Thy sight. Enlighten my eyes less I sleep the sleep of death. Blessed art Thou, O Lord, who enlighteneth all Thy children with Thy glory.

Prayer, Spoken on Seeing a Friend, Restored to
    Health:

Blessed art Thou, O Lord, who hath restored thee to life.

Prayer said on Returning to the Synagogue, after
    having passed safely through Sickness or Danger:

Blessed art Thou, O Lord, who vouchsafeth Thy benefits, to the undeserving, and good unto me.

The Following Prayers are taken from the *Sefer Chayim*, or the Book of Life. (This is a traditional book which contains all the Jewish Laws, Customs and Prayers used in connection with Sickness, Death, Funeral and Mourning.)

The following Scriptural Verses, contained in The
    Book of Life, are spoken on entering a sick room:

"And the Lord will take away from thee all sickness, and he will put none of the evil diseases, which thou knowest upon thee, but will lay them upon all that hate thee. (Deut. 8 : 13.) And he said, if thou wilt diligently hearken to the voice of the Lord Thy God, and will do that which is right in His eyes, and wilt give ear to His commandments, and keep all His statutes, I will put none of the diseases upon thee which I have put upon the Egyptians, for I am the Lord that *healeth* thee. (Ex. 15 :26.) He createth the fruit of the lips, Peace, Peace to him that is far off, and to him that is near, sayeth the Lord, and I will *heal* him." (Is. 57 : 19.)

On Leaving a Sick Room, the Visitor says to the Sick Person:

May God send thee a speedy and perfect cure with all the sick of His people, Israel.

On the Sabbath or Festivals, On Visiting the Sick, One says:

It is the Sabbath (or Festival), and one may not engage in sorrowful prayer. May Thy *healing* be near with all the sick of Israel.

The Prayer said by a Sick Person:

A prayer of the afflicted when he fainteth and poureth out his complaint before the Lord. Hear my prayer, O Lord, and let my cry come unto Thee. Hide not Thy face from me in the day of my distress. Incline Thine ear unto me.

In the day when I call, answer me speedily.

I beseech Thee, O Lord, *Healer of all flesh* to have mercy upon me and support me upon the bed of my sickness, for I am weak.

Send me and all who are sick among Thy children relief and cure. Assuage my pain and renew my youth as the eagle's.

Vouchsafe unto the physician that he may cure my wound, so that my health may spring forth speedily. Hear my prayer, prolong my life, let me complete my years in happiness, that I may be enabled to serve Thee and keep Thy statutes with a perfect heart. Give me understanding to know that this bitter trial has come upon me for my own welfare, so that I may not despise Thy chastening, nor weary of Thy reproof. Amen.

The Prayer of a Sick Man Repenting of his Sin:

O God of forgiveness, who art gracious and merciful, slow to anger and rich in kindness, I confess unto Thee with a broken and contrite heart that I have sinned and done that which is evil in Thy sight. Behold, I repent of my evil way, and return to Thee with a perfect repentance.

Help me that I may not again turn unto folly, but walk before thee in truth and uprightness. Rejoice the soul of Thy servant, for unto Thee do I lift up my soul. *Heal me, O Lord, and I shall be healed. Save me and I shall be saved, for Thou art my praise.* Amen.

Confession on a Death Bed:

I acknowledge, O Lord, my God, and the God of my fathers, that both my cure and death are in Thy hands. May it be Thy will to send me a perfect healing. Yet if my death be fully determined by Thee, I will accept it at Thy hand. May my death be an atonement for all the sins of which I have been guilty against Thee.

Vouchsafe unto me the abounding happiness that is treasured up for the righteous. Make known to me the path of life. In Thy presence, is fullness of joy. At Thy right hand, are pleasures forevermore. Thou who art the Father of the fatherless and judge of the widow, protect my beloved kindred with whose soul my soul is knit. Into Thy hands, I commend my spirit. Thou hast redeemed me, O God of truth. Amen.

Passages That Bear on the Truth of Jewish Science

"I AM THAT I AM"

And Moses said unto God, Behold, when I come unto the children of Israel, and shall say unto them, The God of your fathers hath sent me unto you; and they shall say to me, What is His name? what shall I say unto them? And God said unto Moses, I AM THAT I AM: and he said, Thus shalt thou say unto the children of Israel, I AM hath sent me unto you. And God said moreover unto Moses, Thus shalt thou say unto the children of Israel, the Lord, the God of your fathers, the God of Abraham, the God of Isaac, and the God of Jacob, hath sent me unto you: this is my name for ever, and this is my memorial unto all generations. Go, and gather the elders of Israel together, and say unto them, The Lord, the God of your fathers, the God of Abraham, of Isaac, and of Jacob, hath appeared unto me, saying, I have surely visited you, and seen that which is done to you in Egypt: and I have said, I will bring you up out of the affliction of Egypt unto the land of the Canaanite, and the Hittite, and the Amorite, and the Perizzite, and the Hittite, and the Jebusite, unto a land flowing with milk and honey. (Exodus 3:13-17.)

LENGTH OF LIFE FROM KEEPING GOD'S COMMANDMENTS

Now this is the commandment, the statutes, and the ordinances, which the Lord your God commanded to teach you; that ye might do them in the land whither ye go over to possess it; that thou mightest fear the Lord thy God, to keep all his statutes and his commandments, which I command thee, thou, and thy son, and thy son's son, all the days of thy life; and that thy days may be prolonged. Hear therefore, O Israel, and observe to do it; that it may be well with thee, and that ye may increase mightily, as the Lord, the God of thy fathers, hath promised unto thee, in a land flowing with milk and honey. (Deuteronomy 6: 1-3.)

THE MOST IMPORTANT PRAYER IN JUDAISM

Hear, O Israel; the Lord our God, the Lord is one: and thou shalt love the Lord thy God with all thy heart, with all thy soul, and with all thy might. And these words, which I command thee this day, shall be upon thy heart; and thou shalt teach them diligently unto thy children, and shalt speak of them when thou sittest in thy house, when thou walkest by the way, when thou liest down, and when thou risest up; And thou shalt bind them as a sign upon thy hand, and they shall be frontlets between thine eyes. And thou shalt write them upon the door-posts of thy house, and upon thy gates. (Deuteronomy 6: 4-9.)

BLESSING THAT FOLLOWS FROM TRUE FAITH

And it shall come to pass, if thou shalt hearken diligently unto the voice of the Lord thy God, to

observe to do all his commandments which I command
thee this day, that the Lord thy God will set thee on
high above all the nations of the earth: and all these
blessings shall come upon thee, and overtake thee, if
thou shalt hearken unto the voice of the Lord thy God.
Blessed shalt thou be in the city, and blessed shalt
thou be in the field. Blessed shall be the fruit of thy
body, and the fruit of thy ground, and the fruit of thy
beasts, the increase of thy cattle, and the young of thy
flock. Blessed shall be thy basket and thy kneading-
trough. Blessed shalt thou be when thou comest in,
and blessed shalt thou be when thou goest out.
(Deuteronomy 28:1-5.)

TRUE RELIGION IS WITHIN MAN

For this commandment which I command thee this
day, it is not too hard for thee, neither is it far off. It is
not in heaven, that thou shouldest say, Who shall go
up for us to heaven, and bring it unto us, and make us
to hear it, that we may do it? Neither is it beyond the
sea, that thou shouldest say, Who shall go over the sea
for us, and bring it unto us, and make us to hear it,
that we may do it? But the word is very nigh unto
thee, in thy mouth, and in thy heart, that thou mayest
do it. (Deuteronomy 30:11-14.)

LIFE AND GOOD, THE RESULT OF FAITH IN GOD

See, I have set before thee this day life and good,
and death and evil; in that I command thee this day to
love the Lord thy God, to walk in his ways, and to keep
his commandments and his statutes and his
ordinances, that thou mayest live and multiply, and
that the Lord thy God may bless thee in the land

whither thou goest in to possess it. But if thy heart turn away, and thou wilt not hear, but shalt be drawn away, and worship other gods, and serve them; I denounce unto you this day, that ye shall surely perish; ye shall not prolong your days in the land, whither thou passest over the Jordan to go in to possess it. I call heaven and earth to witness against you this day, that I have set before thee life and death, the blessing and the curse: therefore choose life, that thou mayest live, thou and thy seed; to love the Lord thy God, to obey his voice, and to cleave unto him; for this is thy life, and the length of thy days; that thou mayest dwell in the land which the Lord sware unto thy fathers, to Abraham, to Isaac, and to Jacob, to give them. (Deuteronomy 30: 15-20.)

WISDOM BRINGETH LIFE AND PROSPERITY

Happy is the man that findeth wisdom,
And the man that getteth understanding.
For the gaining of it is better than the gaining of silver,
And the profit thereof than fine gold.
She is more precious than rubies:
And none of the things thou canst desire are to be
    compared unto her.
Length of days is in her- right hand;
In her left hand are riches and honor.
Her ways are ways of pleasantness,
And all her paths are peace.
She is a tree of life to them that lay hold upon her:
And happy is every one that retaineth her.
The Lord by wisdom founded the earth;
By understanding he established the heavens.
By his knowledge the depths were broken up,
And the skies drop down the dew.

My son, let them not depart from thine eyes;
Keep sound wisdom and discretion:
So shall they be life unto thy soul,
And grace to thy neck.
Then shalt thou walk in thy way securely,
And thy foot shall not stumble.
When thou liest down, thou shalt not be afraid:
Yea, thou shalt lie down, and thy sleep shall be
    sweet.
Be not afraid of sudden fear,
Neither of the desolation of the wicked, when it
    cometh:
For the Lord will be thy confidence,
And will keep thy foot from being taken.

                     (Proverbs 3: 13-26.)

THE OMNIPRESENT AND OMNIPOTENT GOD

To whom then will ye liken God? or what likeness will ye compare unto him? Have ye not known? have ye not heard? hath it not been told you from the beginning? have ye not understood from the foundations of the earth? It is he that sitteth above the circle of the earth, and the inhabitants thereof are as grasshoppers; that stretcheth out the heavens as a curtain, and spreadeth them out as a tent to dwell in; that bringeth princes to nothing; that maketh the judges of the earth as vanity. To whom then will ye liken me, that I should be equal to him? saith the Holy One. Lift up your eyes on high, and see who hath created these, that bringeth out their host by number; he calleth them all by name; by the greatness of his might, and for that he is strong in power, not one is lacking.

Why sayest thou, O Jacob, and speakest, O Israel, My way is hid from the Lord, and the justice due to me is passed away from my God? Hast thou not known? hast thou not heard? The everlasting God, the Lord, the Creator of the ends of the earth, fainteth not, neither is weary; there is no searching of his understanding. He giveth power to the faint; and to him that hath no might he increaseth strength. Even the youths shall faint and be weary, and the young men shall utterly fall: but they that wait for the Lord shall renew their strength; they shall mount up with wings as eagles; they shall run, and not be weary; they shall walk, and not be faint. (Isaiah 40:18-31.)

GOD, THE ONLY SAVIOUR

But now saith the Lord that created thee, O Jacob, and he that formed thee, O Israel: Fear not, for I have redeemed thee; I have called thee by thy name, thou art mine. When thou passest through the waters, I will be with thee; and through the rivers, they shall not overflow thee: when thou walkest through the fire, thou shalt not be burned, neither shall the flame kindle upon thee. For I am the Lord thy God, the Holy One of Israel, thy savior; I have given Egypt as thy ransom, Ethiopia and Seba in thy stead. Since thou hast been precious in my sight, and honorable, and I have loved thee; therefore will I give men in thy stead, and peoples instead of thy life. Fear not; for I am with thee: I will bring thy seed from the east, and gather thee from the west; I will say to the north, Give up; and to the south, Keep not back; bring my sons from far, and my daughters from the end of the earth; every one that is called by my name, and whom I have created for my glory, whom I have formed, yea, whom I have made.

Bring forth the blind people that have eyes, and the deaf that have ears. Let all the nations be gathered together, and let the peoples be assembled: who among them can declare this, and show us former things? let them bring their witnesses, that they may be justified; or let them hear, and say, It is truth. Ye are my witnesses, saith the Lord, and my servant whom I have chosen; that ye may know and believe me, and understand that I am he: before me there was no God formed, neither shall there be after me. I, even I, am the Lord; and besides me there is no savior. I have declared, and I have saved, and I have showed; and there was no strange god among you: therefore ye are my witnesses, saith the Lord, and I am God. Yea, since the day was, I am he; and there is none that can deliver out of my hand: I will work, and who can hinder it? (Isaiah 43:1-13.)

MORNING PRAYER OF TRUST IN GOD

O Lord, how are mine adversaries increased!
Many are they that rise up against me.
Many there are that say of my soul,
There is no help for him in God.
But thou, O Lord, art a shield about me;
My glory, and the lifter up of my head.
I cry unto the Lord with my voice,
And he answereth me out of his holy hill.
I laid me down and slept;
I awaked; for the Lord sustaineth me.
I will not be afraid of ten thousands of the people
That have set themselves against me round about.
Arise, O Lord; save me, O my God;

For thou hast smitten all mine enemies upon the
    cheek bone;
Thou hast broken the teeth of the wicked.
Salvation belongeth unto the Lord:
Thy blessing be upon thy people.

The Third Psalm.)

EVENING PRAYER OF TRUST IN GOD

Answer me when I call,
O God of my righteousness;
Thou hast set me at large when I was in distress:
Have mercy upon me, and hear my prayer.
O ye sons of men, how long shall my glory be turned
    into dishonor?
How long will ye love vanity, and seek after falsehood?
But know that the Lord hath set apart for himself him
    that is godly;
The Lord will hear when I call unto him.
Stand in awe, and sin not:
Commune with your own heart upon your bed, and be
    still.
Offer the sacrifices of righteousness,
And put your trust in the Lord.
Many there are that say, Who will show us any good?
O Lord, lift thou up the light of thy countenance upon
    us.
Thou hast put gladness in my heart.
More than they have when their grain and their new
    wine are increased.
In peace will I both lay me down and sleep;
For thou, O Lord, alone makest me dwell in safety.

(The Fourth Psalm.)

MAN HAS DIVINE DIGNITY

O Lord, our God,
How excellent is thy name in all the earth,
Who hast set thy glory upon the heavens!
When I consider thy heavens, the work of thy fingers,
The moon and the stars, which thou hast ordained;
What is man, that thou art mindful of him?
And the son of man, that thou visitest him?
Thou hast made him but little lower than the angels,
And crowned him with glory and honor.
Thou madest him to have dominion over the works of
    thy hands;
Thou hast put all things under his feet:
All sheep and oxen,
Yea, and the beasts of the field,
The birds of the heavens, and the fish of the sea,
Whatsoever passeth through the paths of the seas.
O Lord, our God, How excellent is thy name in all the
earth!

(The Eighth Psalm.)

PRAYER FOR HELP IN AFFLICTION

How long, O Lord, wilt thou forget me for ever?
How long wilt thou hide thy face from me?
How long shall I take counsel in my soul,
Having sorrow in my heart all the day?
How long shall mine enemy be exalted over me?
Consider and answer me, O Lord my God;
Lighten mine eyes, lest I sleep the sleep of death;
Lest mine enemy say, I have prevailed against him;
Lest mine adversaries rejoice when I am moved.
But I have trusted in thy loving-kindness;
My heart shall rejoice in thy salvation.

I will sing unto the Lord,
Because he hath dealt bountifully with me.

(The Thirteenth Psalm.)

THE LORD THE PSALMIST'S PORTION IN LIFE AND DELIVERER IN DEATH

Preserve me, O God; for in thee do I take refuge.
O my soul, thou hast said unto the Lord, Thou art my
     God;
I have no good beyond thee.
As for the saints that are in the earth,
They are the excellent in whom is all my delight.
Their sorrows shall be multiplied that give gifts for
     another god.
Their drink-offerings of blood will I not offer,
Nor take their names upon my lips.
The Lord is the portion of mine inheritance and of
     my cup;
Thou maintainest my lot.
The lines are fallen unto me in pleasant places;
Yea, I have a goodly heritage.
I will bless the Lord who hath given me counsel;
Yea, my heart instructeth me in the night seasons.
I have set the Lord always before me:
Because he is at my right hand, I shall not be moved.
Therefore my heart is glad, and my glory rejoiceth:
My flesh also shall dwell in safety.
For thou wilt not leave my soul in the grave,
Neither wilt thou suffer thy holy one to see corruption.
Thou wilt show me the path of life:
In thy presence is fulness of joy;
In thy right hand there are pleasures for evermore.

(The Sixteenth Psalm.)

A PSALM OF FEARLESS TRUST IN GOD

The Lord is my light and my salvation;
Whom shall I fear?
The Lord is the strength of my life;
Of whom shall I be afraid?
When evil-doers came upon me to eat up my flesh,
Even mine adversaries and my foes, they stumbled
    and fell.
Though a host should encamp against me.
My heart shall not fear;
Though war should rise against me,
Even then will I be confident.
One thing have I asked of the Lord, that will I seek
    after:
That I may dwell in the house of the Lord all the
    days of my life,
To behold the beauty of the Lord,
And to inquire in his temple.
For in the day of trouble he will keep me secretly
    in his pavilion:
In the covert of his tabernacle will he hide me;
He will lift me up upon a rock.
And now shall my head be lifted up above mine
    enemies round about me;
And I will offer in his tabernacle sacrifices of joy;
I will sing, yea, I will sing praises unto the Lord.
Hear, O Lord, when I cry with my voice:
Have mercy also upon me, and answer me.
When thou saidest, Seek ye my face; my heart said
    unto thee,
Thy face, O Lord, will I seek.
Hide not thy face from me;
Put not thy servant away in anger;
Thou hast been my help;

Cast me not off, neither forsake me, O God of my \
    salvation.
When my father and my mother forsake me,
Then the Lord will take me up.
Teach me thy way, O Lord,
And lead me in a plain path,
Because of mine enemies.
Deliver me not over unto the will of mine adversaries:
For false witnesses are risen up against me,
And such as breathe out cruelty.
I had fainted, unless I had believed to see the
    goodness of the Lord
In the land of the living.
Wait for the Lord:
Be strong and let thy heart take courage;
Yea, wait thou for the Lord.

                   (The Twenty-Seventh Psalm.)

GOD, THE FOUNTAIN OF LIFE

Thy loving kindness, O Lord, is in the heavens;
Thy faithfulness reacheth unto the skies.
Thy righteousness is like the mountains of God;
Thy judgments are a great deep:
O Lord, thou preservest man and beast.
How precious is thy loving kindness, O God!
Yea, the children of men take refuge under the shadow
    of thy wings.
They shall be abundantly satisfied with the fatness
    of thy house;
And thou wilt make them drink of the river of thy
    pleasures.
For with thee is the fountain of life:
In thy light shall we see light.
O continue thy lovingkindness unto them that know

thee,
And thy righteousness to the upright in heart.
Let not the foot of pride come against me,
And let not the hand of the wicked drive me away.
There are the workers of iniquity fallen:
They are thrust down, and shall not be able to rise.

(Psalm 36: 5-12.)

THE LIVING GOD

As the heart panteth after the water brooks,
So panteth my soul after thee, O God.
My soul thirsteth for God, for the living God:
When shall I come and appear before God?
My tears have been my food day and night,
While they continually say unto me, Where is thy
    God?
These things I remember, and pour out my soul
    within me,
How I went with the throng, and led them to the
    house of God,
With the voice of love and praise, a multitude keeping
    holyday.
Why art thou cast down, O my soul?
And why art thou disquieted within me?
Hope thou in God; for I shall yet praise him
For the help of his countenance.
O my God, my soul is cast down within me:
Therefore do I remember thee from the land of the
    Jordan,
And the Hermons, from the hill Mozar.
Deep calleth unto deep at the noise of thy waterfalls:
All thy waves and thy billows are gone over me.
Yet the Lord will command his lovingkindness in the
    daytime;

And in the night his song shall be with me,
Even a prayer unto the God of my life.
I will say unto God my rock, Why hast thou forgotten
  me?
Why go I mourning because of the oppression of the
  enemy?
As with a sword in my bones, mine adversaries
  reproach me,
While they continually say unto me, Where is thy
  God?
Why art thou cast down, O my soul?
And why are thou disquieted within me?
Hope thou in God; for I shall yet praise him,
Who is the help of my countenance, and my God.

(The Forty-Second Psalm.)

How goodly are thy tabernacles,
O Lord of hosts!
My soul longeth, yea, even fainteth for the courts of
  the Lord;
My heart and my flesh cry out unto the living God.
Yea, the sparrow hath found a house,
And the swallow a nest for herself, where she may
  lay her young,
Even thine altars, O Lord of hosts, My King, and my
  God.
Blessed are they that dwell in thy house:
They will be still praising thee.
Blessed is the man whose strength is in thee;
In whose heart are the highways to Zion.
Passing through the valley of Weeping they make
  it a place of springs;
Yea, the early rain covereth it with blessings.
They go from strength to strength;
Every one of them appeareth before God in Zion.

O Lord, God of hosts! hear my prayer;
Give ear, O God of Jacob.
Behold, O God, our shield,
And look upon the face of thine anointed.
For a day in thy courts is better than a thousand.
I had rather be a doorkeeper in the house of my God,
Than to dwell in the tents of wickedness.
For the Lord God is a sun and a shield:
The Lord will give grace and glory;
No good thing will he withhold from them that
    walk uprightly.
O Lord of hosts,
Blessed is the man that trusteth in thee.

(The Eighty-Fourth Psalm.)

THE PRAYER OF MOSES, THE MAN OF GOD

Lord, thou hast been our dwelling-place
In all generations.
Before the mountains were brought forth,
Or ever thou hadst formed the earth and the world,
Even from everlasting to everlasting thou art God.
Thou turnest man to destruction,
And sayest, Return, ye children of men.
For a thousand years in thy sight
Are but as yesterday when it is past,
And as a watch in the night.
Thou carriest them away as with a flood; they are
    as a sleep:
In the morning they are like grass which groweth up.
In the morning it flourisheth, and groweth up;
In the evening it is cut down, and withereth.
For all our days are passed away in thy wrath:
We bring our years to an end as a sigh.
The days of our years are three-score years and ten,

Or even by reason of strength fourscore years;
Yet is their pride but labor and sorrow;
For it is soon gone, and we fly away.
Who knoweth the power of thine anger,
And thy wrath according to the fear that is due
    unto thee?
So teach us to number our days,
That we may get us a heart of wisdom.
Return, O Lord; how long?
And let it repent thee concerning thy servants.
Oh satisfy us in the morning with thy loving-kindness,
That we may rejoice and be glad all our days.
Make us glad according to the days wherein thou
    hast afflicted us,
And the years wherein we have seen evil.
Let thy work appear unto thy servants,
And thy glory upon their children.
And let the favor of the Lord our God be upon us;
And establish thou the work of our hands upon us;
Yea, the work of our hands establish thou it.

                      (The Ninetieth Psalm.)

SECURITY OF HIM WHO TRUSTS IN THE LORD

He that dwelleth in the secret place of the Most High
Shall abide under the shadow of the Almighty.
I will say of the Lord, He is my refuge and my fortress;
My God, in whom I trust.
For he will deliver thee from the snare of the fowler,
And from the deadly pestilence.
He will cover thee with his pinions,
And under his wings shalt thou take refuge:
His truth is a shield and a buckler.
Thou shalt not be afraid for the terror by night,
Nor of the arrow that flieth by day;

For the pestilence that walketh in darkness,
Nor of the destruction that wasteth at noonday.
A thousand shall fall at thy side,
And ten thousand at thy right hand;
But it shall not come nigh thee.
Only with thine eyes shalt thou behold,
And see the reward of the wicked.
For thou, O Lord, art my refuge!
Thou hast made the Most High thy habitation;
There shall no evil befall thee,
Neither shall any plague come nigh thy tent.
For he will give his angels charge over thee,
To keep thee in all thy ways.
They shall bear thee up in their hands,
Lest thou dash thy foot against a stone.
Thou shalt tread upon the lion and adder;
The young lion and the serpent shalt thou trample
    under foot.
Because he hath set his love upon me, therefore will
I deliver him: I will set him on high, because he hath
    known my name.
He shall call upon me, and I will answer him;
I will be with him in trouble:
I will deliver him, and honor him.
With long life will I satisfy him,
And show him my salvation.

                   (The Ninety-First Psalm.)

PROSPERITY OF HIM THAT FEARS THE LORD

Praise ye the Lord.
Blessed is the man that feareth the Lord,
That delighteth greatly in his commandments.
His seed shall be mighty upon the earth:
The generations of the upright shall be blessed.

Wealth and riches are in his house;
And his righteousness endureth for ever.
Unto the upright there ariseth light in the darkness:
He is gracious, and merciful, and righteous.
Well is it with the man that dealeth graciously and
    lendeth;
He shall maintain his cause in judgment.
For he shall never be moved;
The righteous shall be had in everlasting
    remembrance.
He shall not be afraid of evil tidings;
His heart is firm, trusting in the Lord,
His heart is established, he shall not be afraid,
Until he see his desire upon his adversaries.
He hath dispersed, he hath given to the needy;
His righteousness endureth for ever:
His horn shall be exalted with honor.
The wicked shall see it, and be grieved;
He shall gnash with his teeth, and melt away:
The desire of the wicked shall perish.

                (One Hundred Twelfth Psalm.)

THE LORD PRAISED FOR EXALTING THE HUMBLE

Praise ye the Lord.
Praise, O ye servants of the Lord,
Praise the name of the Lord.
Blessed be the name of the Lord
From this time forth and for evermore.
From the rising of the sun unto the going down of the
    same
The Lord's name is to be praised.
The Lord is high above all nations,
And his glory above the heavens. .

Who is like unto the Lord our God,
That hath his seat on high,
That humbleth himself to behold
The things that are in the heaven and in the earth?
He raiseth up the poor out of the dust,
And lifteth up the needy from the dunghill;
That he may set him with princes,
Even with the princes of his people.
He maketh the barren woman to keep house,
To be a joyful mother of children.
Praise ye the Lord.

(One Hundred Thirteenth Psalm.)

THANKSGIVING FOR GOD'S SAVING GOODNESS

Oh give thanks unto the Lord; for he is good;
For his lovingkindness endureth for ever.
Let Israel now say,
His lovingkindness endureth for ever.
Let the house of Aaron now say,
His lovingkindness endureth for ever.
Let them now that fear the Lord say,
His lovingkindness endureth for ever.
Out of my distress I called upon the Lord:
The Lord answered me and set me in a large place.
The Lord is on my side; I will not fear:
What can man do unto me?
The Lord is on my side among them that help me:
Therefore shall I see my desire upon them that hate
    me.
It is better to trust in the Lord
Than to put confidence in man.
It is better to trust in the Lord
Than to put confidence in princes.
All nations compassed me about:

In the name of the Lord I will triumph.
They compassed me about; yea, they compassed me
    about;
In the name of the Lord I will triumph.
They compassed me about like bees; they are
    quenched as the fire of thorns:
In the name of the Lord I will triumph.
They did thrust sore at me that I might fall;
But the Lord helped me.
The Lord is my strength and song;
And he is become my salvation.
The voice of rejoicing and salvation is in the tents
    of the righteous:
The right hand of the Lord doeth valiantly.
The right hand of the Lord is exalted:
The right hand of the Lord doeth valiantly.
I shall not die, but live,
And declare the works of the Lord.
The Lord hath chastened me;
But he hath not given me over unto death.
Open to me the gates of righteousness:
I will enter into them, and give thanks unto the
    Lord.
This is the gate of the Lord;
The righteous shall enter into it.
I will give thanks unto thee; for thou hast answered
    me,
And art become my salvation.
The stone which the builders rejected
Has become the chief cornerstone.
This is the Lord's doing;
It is marvelous in our eyes.
This is the day which the Lord hath made;
We will rejoice and be glad in it.
Save now, we beseech thee, O Lord:

O Lord, we beseech thee, send now prosperity.
Blessed be he that cometh in the name of the Lord:
We bless you out of the house of the Lord,
Thou art my God, and I will give thanks unto thee:
Thou art my God, I will exalt thee.
Oh give thanks unto the Lord; for he is good;
For his lovingkindness endureth for ever.

> (The One Hundred Eighteenth Psalm.)

GOD, THE KEEPER OF ISRAEL

I will lift up mine eyes unto the hills:
From whence cometh my help?
My help cometh from the Lord,
Who made heaven and earth.
He will not suffer thy foot to be moved:
He that keepeth thee will not slumber.
Behold, he that keepeth Israel
Will neither slumber nor sleep.
The Lord is thy keeper:
The Lord is thy shade upon thy right hand.
The sun shall not smite thee by day,
Nor the moon by night.
The Lord will guard thee from all evil;
He will guard thy soul.
The Lord will guard thy going out and thy coming in
From this time forth and for evermore.

> (The One Hundred Twenty-First Psalm.)

If the Lord had not been on our side,
Let Israel now say,
If the Lord had not been on our side,
When men rose up against us;
Then they had swallowed us up alive,
When their wrath was kindled against us:

Then the waters had overwhelmed us,
The stream had gone over our soul;
Then the proud waters had gone over our soul.
Blessed be the Lord;
Who hath not given us as a prey to their teeth.
Our soul is escaped as a bird out of the snare of the
    fowlers:
The snare is broken, and we are escaped.
Our help is in the name of the Lord,
Who made heaven and earth.

          (One Hundred Twenty-Fourth Psalm.)

CHILDREN, THE HERITAGE OF GOD

Except the Lord build the house,
They labor in vain that build it:
Except the Lord keep the city,
The watchman watcheth in vain.
It is vain for you to rise up early,
To take rest late,
To eat the bread of toil;
For he giveth unto his beloved sleep.
Lo, children are a heritage of the Lord;
And the fruit of the womb is his reward.
As arrows in the hand of a mighty man,
So are the children of youth.
Happy is the man that hath his quiver full of them:
They shall not be put to shame,
When they speak with their enemies in the gate.

         (One Hundred Twenty-Seventh Psalm.)

BLESSEDNESS FROM THE FEAR OF GOD

Blessed is every one that feareth the Lord,
That walketh in his ways.

For thou shalt eat the labor of thy hands:
Happy shalt thou be, and it shall be well with thee.
Thy wife shall be as a fruitful vine,
In the innermost parts of thy house;
Thy children like olive plants,
Round about thy table.
Behold, thus shall the man be blessed
That feareth the Lord.
The Lord bless thee out of Zion:
And see thou the good of Jerusalem all the days of
    thy life.
Yea, thou shalt see thy children's children.
Peace be upon Israel.

                 (One Hundred Twenty-Eighth Psalm.)

THE UNITY OF BRETHREN

Behold, how good and how pleasant it is
For brethren to dwell together in unity!
It is like the precious oil upon the head,
That ran down upon the beard,
Even Aaron's beard;
That came down upon the skirt of his garments;
Like the dew of Hermon,
That cometh down upon the mountains of Zion:
For there the Lord commanded a blessing,
Even life for evermore.

                 (One Hundred Thirty-Third Psalm.)

GOD'S OMNIPRESENCE AND OMNISCIENCE

Lord, thou hast searched me, and known me
Thou knowest my downsitting and mine uprising;
Thou understandest my thought afar off.
Thou searchest out my path and my lying down,

And art acquainted with all my ways.
For there is not a word in my tongue,
But, lo, O Lord, thou knowest it altogether.
Thou hast beset me behind and before,
And laid thy hand upon me.
Such knowledge is too wonderful for me;
It is high, I cannot attain unto it.
Whither shall I go from thy spirit?
Or whither shall I flee from thy presence?
If I ascend into heaven, thou art there:
If I make my bed in Sheol, behold, thou art there.
If I take the wings of the morning,
And dwell in the uttermost parts of the sea;
Even there shall thy hand lead me,
And thy right hand shall hold me.
If I say, Surely the darkness shall overwhelm me,
And the light about me shall be night;
Even the darkness hideth not from thee,
But the night shineth as the day:
The darkness and the light are both alike to thee.
I will give thanks unto thee; for I am fearfully and
    wonderfully made:
Wonderful are thy works;
And this my soul knoweth right well.
My frame was not hidden from thee,
When I was made in secret.
And curiously wrought in the lowest parts of the
    earth.
Thine eyes did see mine unformed substance;
And in thy book they were all written,
Even the days that were ordained for me
When as yet there was none of them.
How precious also are thy thoughts unto me, O God!
How great is the sum of them!
If I should count them, they are more in number

than the sand:
When I awake, I am still with thee.
Search me, O God, and know my heart:
Try me, and know my thoughts;
And see if there be any wicked way in me,
And lead me in the way ever-lasting.

(Psalm 139: 1-18, 22-24.)

PRAISE TO THE CREATOR AND PRESERVER

Rejoice in the Lord, O ye righteous:
Praise is comely for the upright.
Give thanks unto the Lord with the harp:
Sing praises unto him with the psaltery of ten strings.
Sing unto him a new song;
Play skillfully with a loud noise.
For the word of the Lord is right;
And all his work is done in faithfulness.
He loveth righteousness and justice:
The earth is full of the lovingkindness of the Lord.
By the word of the Lord were the heavens made,
And all the host of them by the breath of his mouth.
He gathereth the waters of the sea together as a heap:
He layeth up the deeps in storehouses.
Let all the earth fear the Lord:
Let all the inhabitants of the world stand in awe of
    him.
For he spake, and it was done;
He commanded, and it stood fast.
The Lord bringeth the counsel of the nations to
    nought;
He maketh the thoughts of the peoples to be of no
    effect.
The counsel of the Lord standeth fast for ever,
The thoughts of his heart to all generations.

Blessed is the nation whose God is the Lord,
The people whom he hath chosen for his own
    inheritance.
The Lord looketh from heaven;
He beholdeth all the sons of men;
From the place of his habitation he looketh forth
Upon all the inhabitants of the earth,
He that fashioneth the hearts of them all,
That considereth all their works.
There is no king saved by the multitude of a host:
A mighty man is not delivered by great strength.
A horse is a vain thing for safety;
Neither doth he deliver any by his great power.
Behold, the eye of the Lord is upon them that fear him,
Upon them that hope in his lovingkindness;
To deliver their soul from death,
And to keep them alive in famine.
Our soul hath waited for the Lord:
He is our help and our shield.
For our heart shall rejoice in him,
Because we have trusted in his holy name.
Let thy lovingkindness, O Lord, be upon us,
According as we have hoped in thee.

                           (The Thirty-Third Psalm.)

INDEX OF BIBLICAL PASSAGES TEACHING THE TRUTH OF JEWISH SCIENCE

Genesis 20
Exodus 15; 22; 26
Exodus 23: 20-25
Numbers 12
Deuteronomy 7: 9-15
Deuteronomy 32; 39

I Samuel 5; 6
I Kings 17: 8-24
II Kings 1: 1-17
II Kings 4: 8-37
II Kings 5
II Kings 8: 7-15
II Kings 20: 1-7
Isaiah 19: 19-22
Jeremiah 17: 12-18
Ezekiel 34: 1-6
Ezekiel 37: 1-14
Hosea 6: 1-31
Malachai 4: 1-3
Psalm 6
Psalm 23
Psalm 30
Psalm 38
Psalm 41: 1-3
Psalm 103: 1-5
Psalm 107: 1-16; 19-22
Proverbs 3: 1-8
Proverbs 4: 20-22

INDEX OF BIBLICAL PASSAGES THAT BEAR ON THE TRUTH OF JEWISH SCIENCE

Exodus 3: 13-17
Deuteronomy 6: 1-3
Deuteronomy 6: 4-9
Deuteronomy 28: 1-5
Deuteronomy 30: 11-14
Deuteronomy 30: 15-20
Joshua 1: 1-9
Proverbs 3: 13-26
Isaiah 40: 18-21

Isaiah 43: 1-13
Psalm 3
Psalm 4
Psalm 8
Psalm 13
Psalm 16
Psalm 27
Psalm 33
Psalm 36: 5-12
Psalm 42
Psalm 61
Psalm 63
Psalm 84
Psalm 90
Psalm 91
Psalm 97
Psalm 112
Psalm 113
Psalm 116
Psalm 121
Psalm 124
Psalm 127
Psalm 128
Psalm 133
Psalm 139: 1-18; 23-24
Psalm 144
Psalm 147